B

Vows and Observances

Berkeley Hills Books
Titles by M. K. Gandhi

The Bhagavad Gita According to Gandhi

Book of Prayers

Prayer

Vows and Observances

The Way to God

Vows and Observances

MOHANDAS K. GANDHI

Edited by John Strohmeier
Foreword by Arun Gandhi
Introduction by Michael N. Nagler

Berkeley Hills Books
Berkeley, California

Published by
Berkeley Hills Books
P. O. Box 9877
Berkeley, California 94709
(888) 848-7303
www.berkeleyhills.com

Cover design by Elysium, San Francisco.
Cover Photo © CORBIS/Bettman.
Manufactured in the United States of America.
Distributed by Publishers Group West.

1 3 5 7 9 10 8 6 4 2

Library of Congress Cataloging-in-Publication Data
(Available from the publisher.)

Contents

Foreword, by Arun Gandhi   9
Introduction, by Michael N. Nagler   11

The Eleven Observances (1928)   29

Maxims of Life: 35
The Ashram Vows (1916)

A History of the Satyagraha Ashram (1932)   49

From Yeravda Mandir:
Essays on the Observances (1930)
    Truth   119
    Ahimsa or Love   122
    Brahmacharya or Chastity   125
    Control of the Palate   128
    Non-Stealing   130
    Non-Possession   133
    Fearlessness   135
    Removal of Untouchability   137
    Bread Labor   139
    Equality of Religions   141
    Humility   145
    The Importance of Vows   147
    Yajna or Sacrifice   149
    Swadeshi   154

Publisher's Note

Beginning in 1904, when Gandhi established Phoenix Farm outside Durban, South Africa, up until his death in 1948, when his home was Sevagram Ashram in Wardha, India, Gandhi lived almost continuously in religious communities which he founded and led. As a result of this experience, he developed rules for community living, which he sometimes summarized as "The Eleven Observances." *Vows and Observances* brings together four texts, written between 1916 and 1932 while he lived at Satyagraha Ashram in Sabarmati, in which Gandhi introduces and comments upon these guidelines for daily living.

We would like to express our thanks to the Navajivan Trust, Ahmedabad, India, for their assistance and permission to reprint these works; and to Vandana Shiva and Eknath Easwaran, who, through their ideas and writings, inspired this effort to bring the thought of Mahatma Gandhi to Western readers.

Foreword

ARUN GANDHI

One day during my early teen years, I got into a playful argument with my sister, Sita. For six months, she said, she would eat just one meal a day. I made light of the vow.

"That is easy. Anybody can do that." Sita caught the bait and retorted, "Well, why don't you take a vow and show us what you can do?"

"Sure," I boasted. "I can live for a whole week on bananas and milk." It was an idle boast. I had no intention of carrying it out. Our parents, who were watching the repartee, were curious to see where it would end, and the moment I made my boastful remark Mother decided to teach me a lesson.

"I take it that is your vow?" she said. "You will now have to undertake it." I was trapped.

In the Hindu tradition of our family, a vow is sacred. Once you utter it, you have to go through with it. There was no escape. So the following week I lived on nothing but bananas and milk, and for several months thereafter, I couldn't stand the sight of bananas and milk.

The taking of vows is a part of Hindu practice, but it is also a universal form of personal discipline. It prepares one for adversity. So one takes a vow to give up something that is very precious. It also teaches one to value one's word, because once you have taken a vow, there is no one watching to see whether you observe it diligently or not except your own conscience.

Mohandas Gandhi grew up in a family where vows were observed daily. In his autobiography, he tells of the time his mother vowed to eat only after she had seen the moon. This vow was taken during the monsoon period in India when the sky may be overcast for weeks. She was so diligent that she remained hungry for days, and this disturbed young Mohan. He would sit at the window praying that the clouds would scatter even for a few minutes so his mother could see the moon. There were times when he would desperately call out to his mother after sighting the moon, but before she could come to the window it would be shrouded by clouds.

These experiences influenced him strongly, and he made the taking of vows a normal practice in the ashrams he created in India and South Africa. He defined the ashram rules as "vows" so that each individual was morally responsible for observing them. There was no need to appoint an enforcer.

It is easy to make a dogma of the wisdom that Gandhi has imparted in this and other writings. But as a wise man has said, "The easiest way to kill a philosophy is to write a book." Once it is enshrined in black and white, it becomes rigid and incontrovertible. Perhaps this is why Gandhi wrote so few books. He was a prolific writer but wrote fewer than five books. He said, "My life is my message," because he wanted people to continue his experiments with truth. This book, therefore, might be read not as one might read the Western Ten Commandments, whose spirit it recalls, but as the notes of a scientist recording the insights of a long and passionate search for truth.

Introduction

MICHAEL N. NAGLER

Gandhi Sutras

While Mahatma Gandhi was in some ways a brilliant theorist, he was primarily a man of action. An idea that could not be put into practice for human betterment held no interest for him, and was not in the strictest sense true. For eighteen years, from its founding on May 20, 1915 until its disbanding on July 26, 1933, the most intense laboratory for that truth was the spiritual community Gandhi set up in his native state of Gujarat, Satyagraha Ashram.

As his close English friend, C. F. Andrews, wrote, "It is impossible to understand Mahatma Gandhi's principles in their entirety without studying their embodiment in his Ashram, or place of spiritual retreat." Andrews goes on: "In India every great moral and spiritual leader sooner or later founds what is called an Ashram for the sake of giving a concrete expression to his own creative ideas." Thus this collection of writings, based on Gandhi's lived experience with the community that was his home, the laboratory of his social experiments and the headquarters for the freedom struggle he directed, brings us as close as the printed page can to the fire of creativity in which he struggled to realize his dream of making India not only free but happy. Here the mature Gandhi, who dared to pit himself against the greatest empire the world had ever seen, drew to himself the family of seekers and activists who would attempt to create the utopia of Rama Rajya, the rule of God.

The result can be felt on every page of the present collection. The first section, "The Eleven Observances," gives condensed definitions of Gandhi's key principles. I know of nothing else in the one-hundred-odd volumes of his *Collected Works* that can bring us into the presence of his mind with such formula-like, scientific clarity. We might call this the Gandhi Sutras. "Maxims of Life," part two, elaborates these key principles and gives some of the reasoning behind them. It is very much in the flavor of the oral setting in which it was delivered, at a talk in Delhi in 1916. Third is the surviving fragment of the "History of Satyagraha Ashram." This text would have been a treasure of history if Gandhi had ever had the time to finish it, but after 1926 "his life was his message." This brief fragment allows us to glimpse some of the experiments that shaped the institutions of the ashram. Part four, "From Yeravda Mandir," although composed as letters to ashram members, was prepared with a larger audience in mind and edited for distribution in several languages. So part one defines, part two "unpacks," part three contextualizes, and part four moves to a greater community what is in effect the rule of Satyagraha Ashram.

If one had time to read only one small collection of Gandhi's writings, then, this would be the one. Yet there is another reason it speaks to us with such immediacy in America today, and that is the long tradition here of experimental communities committed to an ideal way of life.

In 1681, for example, Charles II granted the Quaker William Penn a charter to the vast territory that now bears his name. From about that time until the last Friends legislators threw in the towel during the French and Indian war of 1756, the area we call Pennsylvania was a kind of vast utopian experiment built on Quaker principles. Capital punishment, meted out to 112 infractions under English law, was drastically reduced. The criminal justice system was shifted from a punitive to a restorative character. Workhouses, "whereof one shall be established in every county," replaced prisons. Religious toleration was extended to virtually all sects and creeds.

Penn's relations with the Delaware Indians were almost unimaginable for even our own century, let alone the seventeenth. "I am very sensible of the unkindness and injustice that hath been too much exercised toward you by the people of these parts of the world," Penn wrote to his indigenous subjects, " but I have great love and regard toward you, and I desire to win and gain your love and friendship, by a kind, just and peaceable life." And there was no army. History knows this seventy-year oasis of reason as the "Holy Experiment," a name that would fit Satyagraha Ashram perfectly.

Such a dream seems very remote from us today. But it can never be very far from our desires. No one, least of all in this land of utopian experiments, can entirely forget the dream of a happy community, particularly at a time like this, when life is becoming faster and more frustrating in a way that is seemingly irreversible and out of control. The further the dream slips away, the more we long to recall it, however unconsciously. According to a recent study, fewer than forty percent of Americans think that the country as a whole is going toward a bright future. "Computers probably help," replies one mother, "but what are the children learning now? Are they learning to socialize with other people? . . . Are they going to church?" "Parents don't have time for their children and you can't trust anybody," says another man. "There's more money, but less human caring," adds a government worker from Orchard Park,

New York.

The more one gets to know Gandhi, the more one realizes that human caring, or what he himself called his "insatiable love of mankind" is the drive that underlies all his activities. It runs, unmistakable and consistent, through everything he wrote, and is the most efficient explanation of everything he thought. Gandhi seems to have felt with extraordinary intensity what theologians sometimes call the "brokenness" of the world and what lay people term alienation. Even as a child, he could not endure the coarse brutality with which people treated each other. And as a young man, when he was thrown from a train because of his color during his first week in South Africa, he vowed he would never cease from fighting against "man's inhumanity to man."

In India, that vow became a way of life. He could not tolerate the wall of separation between himself and the poor, so he adopted their poverty. He could not abide the galling Englishman's superiority, so he invented a way of deposing him from that superiority without leaving a residue of rancor. He hated the ever-widening gulf between upper-class professionals and the humble *kisan* (peasant), so he enshrined "bread labor" in his economic system. We think of bread labor as economics, but it is easier to understand as an expression of his thirst for human unity—as is his economic system, as is his politics, his healthcare, and his spirituality.

We learn in this book that he worked to restore India's network of indigenous languages not only, as one may think, to assert India's culture against Western domination and her freedom against Western hegemony, but to restore the living connection between the villager and the learned scientist, who now thought and wrote only in English. As time went on, he devoted more and more of his energy, invested every bit of his prestige, in preventing the drifting apart of Hindu and Muslim and purifying the Hindu caste system of untouchability. All these "vows and observances" are designed to heal that hurting indifference which keeps one human being from another: "There is no room in the ashram for any ideas of high and low."

These ideas speak for themselves, but, as Andrews says, for a full appreciation of them we need to keep in mind the laboratory in which they were tested and, in some cases, discovered. Rather than railing against the awful brokenness of the world, Gandhi's way was to create a world without it. In the microcosm of Satyagraha Ashram—and it was not a small community, at its height there were 250 residents—human caring was reflected in every arrangement. Miraculously, there was time for everyone. One of the most consistent reports we have from residents and visitors is that despite the mind-numbing pace of his activities, Gandhi nourished personal relationships with every person who came to him, and thus encouraged them to have such relationships with one another. They were aiming high.

"The ashram holds . . . that society can be built up on the foundations of ahimsa [nonviolence]."

We should not let the quietness of this statement belie its revolutionary significance. We live today in a world that is founded—without much exaggeration—on violence. It is the incessant message of our mass media (which is to say, our culture), and the ultimate sanction for domestic tranquillity and international peace. We seem to be trying, increasingly, to base institutions on the ultimate threat or use of violence, as though that were the only way to contain disorder, punish crime and assert individual rights. A world based on ahimsa would turn our most fundamental institutions upside down—or rather, put them back on their feet.

In the microcosm of Satyagraha Ashram, this experiment was actually performed, not taking the supposed limits of human nature for an answer. Crime and punishment is a telling example. Occasionally, people committed serious errors at the ashram. How could there not be lapses when such demands of discipline and sacrifice were made of people? But punishment was ruled out—that's part of the violent approach. What was Gandhi to do? He arrived at the solution early on, and it worked perfectly: whenever anyone committed a major moral infraction he took the penance upon himself.

Likewise, to maintain domestic, and eventually even international order—in other words, to carry his experiments far beyond the borders of the community—he proposed a "peace army" of volunteers committed to nonviolent discipline and, where necessary, interposition and sacrifice. Today this is one of the fastest-growing concepts in peace development. Satyagraha Ashram was not just counter-cultural. It was the beginning of a different civilization.

Ahimsa, nonviolence, is the key to this new civilization. For Gandhi, ahimsa went far deeper than mere abstention from physically injuring someone. As he says several times in this book, it is not only pulling your punches but the *conversion of the desire to injure* that generated ahimsa.

If we resent a friend's action or the so-called enemy's action, we still fall short of this doctrine. But when

I say we should not resent, I do not say that we should acquiesce; but by resenting I mean wishing that some harm [*himsa*] should be done to the enemy, or that he should be put out of the way, not even by any action of ours, but by the action of somebody else, or, say, by divine agency. If we harbor even this thought, we depart from this doctrine of ahimsa. Those who join the ashram have to literally accept that meaning.

While we have grown accustomed to a world where we rush into litigation at the first sign of difference, Gandhi called on lawyers to resign unless they saw, as he had seen in 1894, that the true purpose of the law is "to unite parties riven asunder." Where we pursue wealth at the expense of relationships, he pursued relationships at the expense of every excess of wealth. And where we throw up our hands at injustice, he mounted such a determined resistance, that when it was over, not only India, but an entire colonial world, had stepped out of its chains.

Even the happiness felt by residents and, for that matter, visitors to Satyagraha Ashram had a great deal to do with this mighty project. But we should not allow the word "utopian" to mislead us. It turns out that the key to human happiness is not a vacation on Maui, as commercial civilization proclaims, but having meaningful work to do. Life at the ashram was spare, tough, dangerous and all-consuming. And it was also idyllic. There is nothing inaccurate, for example, in this description of the ashram in full swing by a Western visitor:

Morning and evening prayers form one of the features of the common life of the Ashram. All the men, women and children are gathered together, the stars shining above, the river silver in the moonlight, Mahatma Gandhi as discipline personified and yet the very embodiment of love.

At the same time, though, the Mahatma was tough as nails on himself and only a tad less so on those closest to him. His devoted secretary Pyarelal wrote a ditty to the effect that,

> To live with the saints in heaven is a matter of bliss
>   and glory;
> But to live with one on earth, is quite another story.

Anyone who has lived in an ashram can appreciate this.

The St. Benedict of India

In order to understand how we can benefit from his tough experiments, it is helpful to sort out, in the spirit of Gandhi's crowning concept, swadeshi, what aspects of Satyagraha Ashram were keyed to specifically Indian culture and which were universally applicable. Gandhi's definition of an ashram was "group life lived in a religious spirit," but should we think of his ashram as a monastery? A commune? A school for revolution? It turns out that Satyagraha Ashram was all of the above, but also more.

Although Gandhi was happy to own that, "its arrangements involve to a certain extent a deliberate imitation of life in the West," Satyagraha Ashram was the reinvention of an institution as old as anything we know about India's civilization. This is in fact typical of almost all his seemingly new innovations, including Satyagraha (or nonviolence) itself. Gandhi based the ashram's core practices, for example, in the *yamas* and *niyamas*, or "dos and don'ts" that had been codified by Patañjali, probably a contemporary of the Buddha.

The traditional forest ashram, where a revered sage, married or unmarried, gathered around him or herself students for at least twelve years of service and study, however idealized, was the cornerstone of ancient India's educational system and is still today in many ways the very image of Indian civilization. That civilization was founded, remarkably, on the supreme science, *brahmavidya*, or self-realization. This science, otherwise known as yoga or meditation, is next to impossible to pursue in cities or universities, and there seem to be only a few rare types who can carry it out on their own in hermitages or caves.

The ideal setting for this discipline was always a small, loving community leading a settled life in a peaceful, natural environment—an ashram. The earliest descriptions of these vibrant centers of human struggle and development (the word *ashrama* means place of exertion) portray them as the setting for the "forest sessions" recorded in the ancient Upanishads, and the spirit of those texts does sometimes strangely foreshadow that of the rebellious Mahatma so many centuries later.

Indian ashrams differed from Western monasteries in typically Indian ways. For one thing, the preceptor was often married (like a Rabbi) and he or she could have women as well as men students, making an environment more like an extended family than an intentional community. There have been strictly monastic communities in India, particularly under Buddhist influence, but in others sexual purity was maintained more by meditation and the example of the teacher than by the geographical removal of temptation. Normally an ashram (as far as we know) did not have a written rule, and the existence of this book may be one of those things Gandhi claimed were owed to a Western model. More importantly, the ashram was its own site of experimentation and had no affiliation with any central authority somewhere else. Swadeshi applied here as well. Despite these differences, ashram and monastery had (and have) the same purpose, and that purpose is twofold: to provide an environment for intense spiritual development, and to serve as a model of loving community for the turbulent world around it. The monastic redoubt of the Western Middle Ages was isolated from the workaday world, but it was also a city on the hill for that world. Both monastery and ashram are supposed to look both inward to its members, and outward to the world around them.

We do well to keep in mind, however, the biggest difference. The traditional ashram, sometimes referred to as a *gurukula* or "teacher's family," revolves around that teacher, who is supposed to be an illumined person. There is no Rome in Hindu or Buddhist India. Spiritual authority is vested in the teacher him or herself, and arises entirely from what he or she has achieved. At one time, the Christian system was not so different. "It is difficult for a modern reader to enter into the intensity of the *didaskaleion*, of the small study-circle of male and female disciples that would gather for years around a single spiritual guide" in the first three centuries after Jesus, Peter Brown reminds us. In his book, *The Body and Society in Late Antiquity*, he writes, "A Christian bishop traveled regularly all the way from Cappadocia . . . to Palestine, in order to deepen his spiritual life by sitting at the feet of the great Origen," the way hundreds of thousands of devotees flock to see an Anandamayi Ma or a Swami Ramdas today. "There were many serious Christians who were convinced that only through prolonged, intimate contact with a spiritual guide" would religion come to life for them. The main point of going to an ashram was to have that prolonged and intimate contact with an illumined person. This has long been held indispensable in India for one's spiritual development.

Whatever caused this reliance on personal contact, or *darshan*, to subside in the West, knowing that it did not subside in India helps us understand why Gandhi hesitated before using the word "ashram" for his community. In South Africa twenty years earlier it had been Phoenix Farm, and Tolstoy Settlement. Not until he reached the banks of the Sabarmati in 1915 did he "come out" with the word ashram. That is because in so doing he was implicitly accepting the role of a spiritual teacher. This is not done lightly in India. Gandhi did not actually allow anyone, as far as we know, to take formal initiation from him or regard him or herself as his student— he fought shy of all that. But his implicit adoption of that responsibility should always be in our minds when we ask what kind of institution it was, the role it was intended to play in the freedom struggle and the much larger revolution against industrial civilization—and how far and in what ways we can learn from the life of Satyagraha Ashram.

Highlander Folk School

There was another rather striking difference, of course, between Satyagraha Ashram and any monastery we may be familiar with, be it medieval or modern. Most of them have not been the headquarters of a revolution.

Reading this particular collection of texts, it is easy to forget that such earth-shaking events are being prepared by the life of prayer and discipline in the ashram. With quiet understatement, Gandhi explains that the institution "set out to remedy what it thought were defects in our national life from the religious, economic and political standpoints." At the time (1916), he did not expect a major Satyagraha action for at least five years. But he knew perfectly well that rebuilding the village economy, creating a new educational system and so forth, was putting India on a collision course with the "paramount power" and preparing confrontations that were destined, some day, to break the British connection, which had been a locked-down colonial occupation since the Battle of Plassey in 1757. There had been uprisings before, but this time, India would stage the fight on her own terms. For perhaps the first time in history, a battle of vast significance would be fought with a different kind of power.

Little is said about this turmoil in these pages, and reading them you would hardly realize that the ashram was the storm-center of one of the most profound upheavals of the twentieth century—not to mention that its founder was causing them. Almost the only hint of the storms breaking on the ashram walls comes within Gandhi's explanation that the children are taught politics almost from infancy, so that they can understand how "the country is vibrating with new emotions, with new aspirations, with a new life." (Though he characteristically doesn't mention that he himself and the ashram itself are the source of that new life).

This impression of calm is not misleading, it is actually quite significant. Gandhi was the eye of the storm; that's what prayer had done for him. There was a deep center of peace within him that no turmoil could shake—and he occasioned more turmoil than most men of even this fractious century. When ashram residents learned gradually to turn inwards and find the resources within themselves, they were simultaneously being "trained in the moral and emotional controls essential for a Satyagrahi, so that his [or her] grip would not give way to hatred or violence, even under provocation." B. R. Nanda writes that by the time of the great Salt March of 1930 (the climax of the freedom struggle), Sabarmati "was . . . assuming the role which Phoenix and Tolstoy Ashrams had done in South Africa: it became the recruiting ground for the vanguard of freedom and a hub of political activities." One of the attractions of its site, after all, had been its proximity to Sabarmati jail. On their evening walks, ashramites strode passed its gates.

Ms. Rosa Parks was featured by *Time Magazine* this year as one of the hundred most influential people of the century. The article pointed out that whereas most Americans think of Rosa Parks as a demure, pleasant-enough seamstress who backed into history by being too tired to get out of her seat on a bus one day, in reality she had been trained in nonviolence spirit and tactics at a famous institution, Highlander Folk School. It seems to be a difficult concept for most of us that peace is a skill that can be learned. We know *war* can be learned, but we seem to think that one becomes a peacemaker by a mere change of heart. No one who lived with Gandhi, who had himself learned "from bitter experience" day in and day out for more two decades what it takes to conserve anger, would make that mistake. Peace can be learned, and it has to be learned, and that learning doesn't come easily to anyone.

The conquest of violence precedes all other conquests;

and the hardest thing to learn about this conquest is that it's the conquest of our own violence that comes first. It is primarily at the ashram, then, that volunteers were trained to endure prison, to face hatred with love and come off victorious. They were in daily preparation for those moments when, as writer Marshall Frady put it so beautifully, "in the catharsis of a live confrontation with wrong, when an oppressor's violence is met with a forgiving love, he can be vitally touched, and even, at least momentarily, reborn as a human being, while the society witnessing such a confrontation will be quickened in conscience toward compassion and justice."

If the Empire had been made on the playing fields of Eton and Harrow, its long overdue downfall was being prepared in little cottages and prayer meetings by the banks of the Sabarmati.

Womb of the Future

During the "Great Fast" of September, 1924, when the Hindu-Muslim unity he had achieved in the early phase of non-cooperation came apart disastrously, and riots, particularly at Kohat, left him in agony, Gandhi reaffirmed the purpose of his life in these words:

What if we have [different] bodies? We have but one soul. The rays of the sun are many through refraction. But they have the same source. I cannot, therefore, detach myself from the wickedest soul, nor may I be denied identity with the most virtuous. Whether, therefore, I will or not, I must involve in my own experiment the whole of my kind. Nor can I do without experiment. Life is but an endless series of experiments.

These experiments did not come to an end when he disbanded the ashram in 1933 as an act of renunciation and a gesture of defiance toward the Government, which had been harrassing them for nonpayment of taxes: "The disbandment of the ashram would mean that every inmate of it would constitute a walking ashram, carrying with him or her the responsibility for realizing the ashram ideal, no matter where situated, whether in prison or outside." It was his deep faith, shared by all practitioners of principled nonviolence, that no act of Truth can fail to have its beneficial effects, whether or not we see them with our limited, human vision.

In one of Gandhi's favorite parables from Hindu mythology, the boy, Prahlad, infuriated his demon father by his unswerving love for God. But when he patiently endured his father's wrath,

> Truth rose triumphant. Not that Prahlad suffered the tortures because he knew that some day or other in his very lifetime he would be able to demonstrate the infallibility of the law of Truth; that fact was there. But if he had died in the midst of torture, he would still have adhered to Truth. That is the Truth that I would like us to follow.

"The results of my experiments," he elsewhere said, "lie in the womb of the future."

We are that future. For even when Satyagraha Ashram was operating as such, the results of its experiments were designed to be copied all over India, and what he told his fellow Indians applies, *mutatis mutandis*, to us. "I am not here asking you to crowd into the ashram, there is no room there. But I say that every one of you may enact that ashram life individually and collectively. I shall be satisfied with anything that you may choose from the rules I have ventured to place before you and act up to it."

If this story reawakens the dream of happiness and loving community that was once so characteristically American, there is one part of his vast experiments we dare not forget. We must not forget that for him the experiment of life was primarily spiritual. Even the forms of worship he worked out with his community were arrived at, with their precise adjustment of individual needs to communal creativity, by experiment. He found, for example, that even though his head told him God has no form, no limiting attributes, "My intellect can exercise no influence over my heart. I am prepared to admit that my heart in its weakness hankers after a God with attributes." Even in India, with her priceless spiritual heritage, religion must be experimented on and practiced.

Note the delicate irony, very Gandhian, with which he alludes to his own role in this:

> Our scriptures have laid down certain rules as maxims of life and as axioms which we have to take for granted as self-demonstrated truths. . . . Believing in these implicitly for all these long years and having *actually endeavored to reduce to practice* these injunctions of the shastras [scriptures], I have deemed it necessary to seek the association of those who think with me in founding this institution.

Many of the experiments discovered or worked out at Satyagraha Ashram have already made their way, suitably adapted, into post-modern life. The late E. F. Schumacher once confided in me that his "appropriate technology" movement had grown out of Gandhi's spinning wheel. As mentioned above, his concept of a "peace army" is slowly being nudged into life by experimenters around the world. But if we want to live in a solid, stable community of relationships, if not in an actual intentional community; if we want to live for a high purpose, like building world peace, and be strong enough to work through the resistance that living for a positive goal will rouse in the present world order — above all if we want to ground a meaningful, humanized life in some meaningful spirituality, then Gandhi's relentless experiments have much more to teach us. And this book is one of the best ways to learn about them.

The Eleven Observances

The explanation of the eleven observances given here is taken from the Constitution of Satyagraha Ashram, the spiritual community Gandhi founded in 1915, and where he lived throughout much of his adult life. The Constitution was first drafted in 1915, and revised to this form in 1928.

OBJECT

The object of this ashram is that its members should qualify themselves for, and make a constant endeavor towards, the service of the country, not inconsistent with the universal welfare.

OBSERVANCES

The following observances are essential for the fulfillment of the above object:

I. Truth

Truth is not fulfilled by mere abstinence from telling or practicing an untruth in ordinary relations with fellow-men. But Truth is God, the one and only Reality. All other observances take their rise from the quest for, and the worship of, Truth. Worshippers of Truth must not resort to untruth, even for what they may believe to be the good of the country, and they may be required civilly to disobey even the orders of parents and elders in virtue of their paramount loyalty to Truth.

II. Non-violence, or Love

Mere non-killing is not enough. The active part of non-violence is love. The law of Love requires equal consideration for all life from the tiniest insect to the highest man. One who follows this law must not be angry even with the perpetrator of the greatest imaginable wrong, but must love him, wish him well and serve him. Although he must thus love the wrongdoer, he must never submit to his wrong or his injustice, but must oppose it with all his might, and must patiently and without resentment suffer all the hardships to which the wrongdoer may subject him in punishment for his opposition.

III. Chastity (Brahmacharya)

Observance of the foregoing principles is impossible without the observance of celibacy. It is not enough that one should not look upon any woman or man with a lustful eye; animal passion must be so controlled as to be excluded even from the mind. If married, one must not have a carnal mind regarding one's wife or husband, but must consider her or him as one's lifelong friend, and establish a relationship of perfect purity. A sinful touch, gesture or word is a breach of this principle.

IV. Control of the Palate

The observance of brahmacharya has been found, from experience, to be extremely difficult so long as one has not acquired mastery over taste. Control of the palate has, therefore, been placed as a principle by itself. Eating is necessary only for sustaining the body and keeping it a fit instrument for service, and must never be practiced for self-indulgence. Food must, therefore, be taken, like medicine, under proper restraint. In pursuance of this principle, one must eschew exciting foods, such as spices and condiments. Meat, liquor, tobacco, *bhang,* etc., are excluded from the ashram. This principle requires abstinence from feasts or dinners which have pleasure as their object.

V. Non-stealing

It is not enough not to take another's property without his permission. One becomes guilty of theft even by using differently anything which one has received in trust for use in a particular way, as well as by using a thing longer than the period for which it has been lent. It is also theft if one receives anything which one does not really need. The fine truth at the bottom of this principle is that Nature provides just enough, and no more, for our daily need.

VI. Non-Possession or Poverty

This principle is really a part of number V. Just as one must not receive, so must one not possess anything which one does not really need. It would be a breach of this principle to possess unnecessary food-stuffs, clothing or furniture. For instance, one must not keep a chair if one can do without it. In observing this principle one is led to a progressive simplification of one's own life.

VII. Physical Labor

Physical labor is essential for the observance of non-stealing and non-possession. Man can be saved from injuring society, as well as himself, only if he sustains his physical existence by physical labor. Able-bodied adults must do all their personal work themselves, and must not be served by others, except for proper reasons. But they must, at the same time, remember that service of children, as well as of the disabled, the old and the sick, is a duty incumbent on every person who has the required strength.

VIII. Swadeshi

Man is not omnipotent. He therefore serves the world best by first serving his neighbor. This is swadeshi, a principle which is broken when one professes to serve those who are more remote in preference to those who are near. Observance of swadeshi makes for order in the world; the breach of it leads to chaos. Following this principle, one must as far as possible purchase one's requirements locally and not buy things imported from foreign lands, which can easily be manufactured in the country. There is no place for self-interest in swadeshi, which enjoins the sacrifice of oneself for the family, of the family for the village, of the village for the country, and of the country for humanity.

IX. Fearlessness

One cannot follow Truth or Love so long as one is subject to fear. As there is at present a reign of fear in the country, meditation on and cultivation of fearlessness have a particular importance. Hence its separate mention as an observance. A seeker after Truth must give up the fear of parents, caste, government, robbers, etc., and he must not be frightened by poverty or death.

X. Removal of Untouchability

Untouchability, which has taken such deep roots in Hinduism, is altogether irreligious. Its removal has therefore been treated as an independent principle. The so-called untouchables have an equal place in the ashram with other classes. The ashram does not believe in caste, which it considers has injured Hinduism, because its implications of superior and inferior status, and of pollution by contact, are contrary to the law of Love. The ashram, however, believes in *varnashrama dharma.*

The division of *varnas* is based upon occupation, and therefore a person should maintain himself by following the hereditary occupation, not inconsistent with fundamental morals, and should devote all his spare time and energy to the acquisition and advancement of true knowledge. The ashramas (the four stages) spoken of in the *smritis* are conducive to the welfare of mankind. Although the ashram believes in *varnashrama dharma,* there is no place in it for distinction of varnas, as the ashram life is conceived in the light of the comprehensive and non-formal sannyasa of the Bhagavad Gita. [For Gandhi's discussion of the varnas, or hereditary professional classes, and the ashramas, or four stages of life, see page 99 ff.]

XI. Tolerance

The ashram believes that the principal faiths of the world constitute a revelation of Truth, but as they have all been outlined by imperfect man, they have been affected by imperfections and alloyed with untruth. One must therefore entertain the same respect for the religious faiths of others as one accords to one's own. Where such tolerance becomes a law of life, conflict between different faiths becomes impossible, and so does all effort to convert other people to one's own faith. One can only pray that the defects in the various faiths may be overcome, and that they may advance, side by side, towards perfection.

Maxims of Life:
The Vows of Satyagraha Ashram

This text is taken from a speech delivered by Gandhi to the Madras Y.M.C.A. and first published in New India, *February 16, 1916. The purpose of this speech was to outline the ethical principles upon which Gandhi founded the Satyagraha Ashram.*

Our scriptures have laid down certain rules as maxims of life and as axioms which we have to take for granted as self-demonstrated truths. The shastras tell us that without living according to those maxims, we are incapable even of having a reasonable perception of religion. Believing in these implicitly for all these long years and having actually endeavored to reduce to practice these injunctions of the *shastras*, I have deemed it necessary to seek the association of those who think with me in founding this institution. And I shall venture this morning to place before you the rules that have been drawn up and that have to be observed by everyone who seeks to be a member of that ashram.

Five of these are known as *yamas*, and the first and the foremost is

The Vow of Truth

Not truth simply as we ordinarily understand it, that as far as possible we ought not to resort to a lie; that is to say, not truth which merely answers the saying, "Honesty is the best policy," implying that if it is not the best policy, we may depart from it. But here Truth, as it is conceived, means that we have to rule our life by this law of Truth at any cost. And in order to satisfy the definition, I have drawn upon the celebrated illustration of the life of Prahlad.

For the sake of Truth, he dared to oppose his own father, and he defended himself not by retaliation, by paying his father back in his own coin, but in defense of Truth, as he knew it, he was prepared to die without caring to return the blows that he had received from his father or from those who were charged with his father's instructions. Not only that, he would not in any way even parry the blows. On the contrary, with a smile on his lips, he underwent the innumerable tortures to which he was subjected, with the result that, at last, Truth rose triumphant. Not that Prahlad suffered the tortures because he knew that some day or other in his very lifetime he would be able to demonstrate the infallibility of the law of Truth; that fact was there. But if he had died in the midst of torture, he would still have adhered to Truth. That is the Truth that I would like us to follow.

There was an incident I noticed yesterday. It was a trifling incident, but I think these trifling incidents are like straws which show which way the wind is blowing. The incident was this: I was talking to a friend who wanted to talk to me aside, and we were engaged in a private conversation. A third friend dropped in and he politely asked whether he was intruding. The friend to whom I was talking said, "Oh, no, there is nothing private here." I felt taken aback a little, because, as I was taken aside, I knew that so far as this friend was concerned, the conversation was private. But he immediately, out of politeness, I would call it over-politeness, said there was no private conversation and that he (the third friend) could join. I suggest to you that this is a departure from my definition of Truth. I think that the friend should have, in the gentlest manner possible, but still openly and frankly, said, "Yes, just now, as you properly say, you would be intruding," without giving the slightest offense to the person if he was himself a gentleman—and we are bound to consider everybody to be a gentleman unless he proves to be otherwise.

But I may be told that the incident, after all, proves the gentility of the nation. I think that it is overproving the case. If we continue to say these things out of politeness, we really become a nation of hypocrites. I recall a conversation I had with an English friend. He was comparatively a stranger. He is a Principal of a college and has been in India for several years. He was comparing notes with me, and he asked me whether I would admit that we, unlike most Englishmen, would not dare to say "No" when it was "No" that we meant. And I must admit that I immediately said "Yes." I agree with that statement. We do hesitate to say "No", frankly and boldly, when we want to pay due regard to the sentiments of the person whom we are addressing. In this ashram, we make it a rule that we must say "No" when we mean "No", regardless of consequences. This, then, is the first rule. Then we come to

The Doctrine of Ahimsa

Literally speaking, ahimsa means non-killing. But to me it has a world of meaning and takes me into realms much higher, infinitely higher, than the realm to which I would go, if I merely understood by ahimsa non-killing. Ahimsa really means that you may not offend anybody, you may not harbor an uncharitable thought even in connection with one who may consider himself to be your enemy.

Pray notice the guarded nature of this thought; I do not say "whom you consider to be your enemy," but "who may consider himself to be your enemy." For one who follows the doctrine of ahimsa, there is no room for an enemy; he denies the existence of an enemy. But there are people who consider themselves to be his enemies, and he cannot help that circumstance. So, it is held that we may not harbor an evil thought even in connection with such persons. If we return blow for blow, we depart from the doctrine of ahimsa.

But I go further. If we resent a friend's action or the so-called enemy's action, we still fall short of this doctrine. But when I say we should not resent, I do not say that we should acquiesce; but by resenting I mean wishing that some harm should be done to the enemy, or that he should be put out of the way, not even by any action of ours, but by the action of somebody else, or, say, by divine agency. If we harbor even this thought, we depart from this doctrine of ahimsa. Those who join the ashram have to literally accept that meaning.

That does not mean that we practice that doctrine in its entirety. Far from it. It is an ideal which we have to reach, and it is an ideal to be reached even at this very moment, if we are capable of doing so. But it is not a proposition in geometry to be learnt by heart: it is not even like solving difficult problems in higher mathematics; it is infinitely more difficult than solving those problems. Many of you have burnt the midnight oil in solving those problems. If you want to follow out this doctrine, you will have to do much more than burn the midnight oil. You will have to pass many a sleepless night, and go through many a mental torture and agony before you can reach, before you can even be within measurable distance of this goal. It is the goal, and nothing less than that, you and I have to reach if we want to understand what a religious life means.

I will not say much more on this doctrine than this: that a man who believes in the efficacy of this doctrine finds in the ultimate stage, when he is about to reach the goal, the whole world at his feet, not that he wants the whole world at his feet, but it must be so. If you express your love—ahimsa—in such a manner that it impresses itself indelibly upon your so-called enemy, he must return that love. Another thought which comes out of this is that, under this rule, there is no room for organized assassinations, and there is no room for murders even openly committed, and there is no room for any violence even for the sake of your country, and even for guarding the honor of precious ones that may be under your charge. After all, that would be a poor defense of honor. This doctrine of ahimsa tells us that we may guard the honor of those who are under our charge by delivering *ourselves* into the hands of the man who would commit the sacrilege. And that requires far greater physical and mental courage than the delivering of blows.

You may have some degree of physical power—I do not say courage—and you may use that power. But after that is expended, what happens? The other man is filled with wrath and indignation, and you have made him more angry by matching your violence against his; and when he has done you to death, the rest of his violence is delivered against your charge. But if you do not retaliate, but stand your ground, between your charge and the opponent, simply receiving the blows without retaliating, what happens? I give you my promise that the whole of the violence will be expended on you, and your charge will be left unscathed. Under this plan of life, there is no conception of patriotism which justifies such wars as you witness today in Europe. Then there is

The Vow of Celibacy

Those who want to perform national service, or those who want to have a glimpse of the real religious life, must lead a celibate life, no matter if married or unmarried. Marriage but brings a woman closer together with the man, and they become friends in a special sense, never to be parted either in this life or in the lives that are to come. But I do not think that, in our conception of marriage, our lusts should necessarily enter. Be that as it may, this is what is placed before those who come to the ashram. I do not deal with that at any length. Then we have

The Vow of the Control of the Palate

A man who wants to control his animal passions easily does so if he control his palate. I fear this is one of the most difficult vows to follow. I am just now coming after having inspected the Victoria Hostel. I saw there, not to my dismay (though it should be to my dismay, but I am used to it now) that there are so many kitchens, not kitchens that are established in order to serve caste restrictions, but kitchens that have become necessary in order that people can have the condiments, and the exact weight of the condiments, to which they are used in the respective places from which they come. And therefore we find that for the Brahmins themselves there are different compartments and different kitchens catering for the delicate tastes of all these different groups.

I suggest to you that this is simply slavery to the palate,

rather than mastery over it. I may say this: Unless we take our minds off from this habit, and unless we shut our eyes to the tea shops and coffee shops and all these kitchens, and unless we are satisfied with foods that are necessary for the proper maintenance of our physical health, and unless we are prepared to rid ourselves of stimulating, heating and exciting condiments that we mix with our food, we will certainly not be able to control the overabundant, unnecessary, exciting stimulation that we may have. If we do not do that, the result naturally is, that we abuse ourselves and we abuse even the sacred trust given to us, and we become less than animals and brutes— eating, drinking and indulging passions we share in common with the animals, but have you ever seen a horse or a cow indulging in the abuse of the palate as we do? Do you suppose that it is a sign of civilization, a sign of real life, that we should multiply our eatables so far that we do not even know where we are, and seek dish after dish until at last we have become absolutely mad and run after the newspaper sheets which give us advertisements about these dishes? Then we have

The Vow of Non-Thieving

I suggest that we are thieves in a way. If I take anything that I do not need for my own immediate use, and keep it, I thieve it from somebody else. I venture to suggest that it is the fundamental law of nature, without exception, that nature produces enough for our wants from day to day, and if only everybody took enough for himself and nothing more, there would be no pauperism in this world, there would be no man dying of starvation in this world. But so long as we have got this inequality, so long we are thieving.

I am no socialist and I do not want to dispossess those who have got possessions; but I do say that, personally, those of us who want to see light out of darkness have to follow the rule. I do not want to dispossess anybody. I should then be departing from the rule of ahimsa. If somebody else possesses more than I do, let him. But so far as my own life has to be regulated, I do say that I dare not possess anything which I do not want. In India we have got three millions of people having to be satisfied with one meal a day, and that meal consisting of a chapati containing no fat in it, and a pinch of salt. You and I have no right to anything that we really have until these three million are clothed and fed better. You and I, who ought to know better, must adjust our wants, and even undergo voluntary starvation in order that they may be nursed, fed and clothed. Then there is the vow of non-possession which follows as a matter of course. Then I go to

The Vow of Swadeshi

The vow of swadeshi is a necessary vow. But you are conversant with the swadeshi life and the swadeshi spirit. I suggest to you we are departing from one of the sacred laws of our being when we leave our neighbor and go out somewhere else in order to satisfy our wants. If a man comes from Bombay here and offers you wares, you are not justified in supporting the Bombay merchant or trader so long as you have got a merchant at your very door, born and bred in Madras. That is my view of swadeshi. In your village, so long as you have got your village-barber, you are bound to support him to the exclusion of the finished barber who may come to you from Madras. If you find it necessary that your village-barber should reach the attainment of the barber from Madras, you may train him to that. Send him to Madras by all means, if you wish, in order that he may learn his calling. Until you do that, you are not justified in going to another barber. That is swadeshi.

So, when we find that there are many things that we cannot get in India, we must try to do without them. We may have to do without many things which we may consider necessary, but believe me, when you have that frame of mind, you will find a great burden taken off your shoulders, even as the pilgrim did in that inimitable book, *Pilgrim's Progress:* There came a time when the mighty burden that the pilgrim was carrying on his shoulders unconsciously dropped from him, and he felt a freer man than he was when he started on the journey. So will you feel freer men than you are now, immediately you adopt this swadeshi life. We have also

The Vow of Fearlessness

I found, throughout my wanderings in India, that India—educated India—is seized with a paralyzing fear. We may not open our lips in public; we may not declare our confirmed opinion in public. We may hold those opinions; we may talk about them secretly; and we may do anything we like within the four walls of our house—but those are not for public consumption. If we had taken a vow of silence, I would have nothing to say. When we open our lips in public, we say things which we do not really believe in. I do not know whether this is not the experience of almost every public man who speaks in India.

I then suggest to you that there is only one being, if being is the proper term to be used, whom we have to fear, and that is God. When we fear God, we shall fear no man, no matter how high-placed he may be. And if you want to follow the vow of truth in any shape or form, fearlessness is the necessary consequence. And so you find, in the *Bhagavad Gita*, fearlessness is declared as the first essential quality of a Brahmin. We fear consequences, and therefore we are afraid to tell the truth. A man who fears God will certainly not fear any earthly consequence. Before we can aspire to the position of understanding what religion is, and before we can aspire to the position of guiding the destinies of India, do you not see that we should adopt this habit of fearlessness? Or shall we over-awe our countrymen even as we are over-awed? We thus see how important this fearlessness vow is. And we have also

The Vow Regarding the Untouchables

There is an ineffaceable blot that Hinduism today carries with it. I have declined to believe that it has been handed to us from immemorial times. I think that this miserable, wretched, enslaving spirit of "untouchableness" must have come to us when we were, in the cycle of our lives, at our lowest ebb, and that evil has still stuck to us and it still remains with us. It is, to my mind, a curse that has come to us, and as long as that curse remains with us, so long I think we are bound to consider that every affliction that we labor under in this sacred land is a fit and proper punishment for this great and indelible crime that we are committing. That any person should be considered untouchable because of his calling passes one's comprehension; and you, the student world, who receive all this modern education, if you become a party to this crime, it were better that you received no education whatsoever.

Of course, we are laboring under a very heavy handicap.

Although you may realize that there cannot be a single human being on this earth who should be considered to be untouchable, you cannot react upon your families, you cannot react upon your surroundings, because all your thought is conceived in a foreign tongue, and all your energy is devoted to that. And so we have also introduced a rule in this ashram that we shall receive our

Education Through the Vernaculars

In Europe, every cultured man learns, not only his language, but also other languages, certainly three or four. And even as they do in Europe, in order to solve the problem of language in India, we, in this ashram, make it a point to learn as many Indian vernaculars as we possibly can. And I assure you that the trouble of learning these languages is nothing compared to the trouble that we have to take in mastering the English language. We never master the English language; with some exceptions, it has not been possible for us to do so; we can never express ourselves as clearly as we can in our own mother tongue. How dare we rub out of our memory all the years of our infancy?

But that is precisely what we do when we commence our higher life, as we call it, through the medium of a foreign tongue. This creates a breach in our life for bridging which we shall have to pay dearly and heavily. And you will see now the connection between these two things—education and untouchableness—this persistence of the spirit of untouchableness even at this time of the day in spite of the spread of knowledge and education.

Education has enabled us to see the horrible crime. But

we are seized with fear also and, therefore, we cannot take this doctrine to our homes. And we have got a superstitious veneration for our family traditions and for the members of our family. You say, "My parents will die if I tell them that I, at least, can no longer partake of this crime." I say that Prahlad never considered that his father would die if he pronounced the sacred syllables of the name of Vishnu. On the contrary, he made the whole of that household ring, from one corner to another, by repeating that name even in the sacred presence of his father. And so you and I may do this thing in the sacred presence of our parents. If, after receiving this rude shock, some of them expire, I think that would be no calamity. It may be that some rude shocks of the kind might have to be delivered. So long as we persist in these things which have been handed down to us for generations, these incidents may happen. But there is a higher law of nature, and in due obedience to that higher law, my parents and myself should make that sacrifice. And then we follow

Hand-Weaving

You may ask, "Why should *we* use our hands?" and say, "The manual work has got to be done by those who are illiterate. I can only occupy myself with reading literature and political essays." I think that we have to realize the dignity of labor. If a barber or shoe-maker attends a college, he ought not to abandon the profession of barber or shoe-maker. I consider that a barber's profession is just as good as the profession of medicine.

Last of all, when you have conformed to these rules, I think then, and not till then, you may come to

Politics

and dabble in them to your heart's content, and certainly you will then never go wrong. Politics, divorced of religion, have absolutely no meaning. If the student-world crowd the political platforms of this country, to my mind it is not necessarily a healthy sign of national growth; but that does not mean that you, in your student-life, ought not to study politics. Politics are a part of our being; we ought to understand our national institutions, and we ought to understand our national growth and all those things. We may do it from our infancy. So, in our ashram, every child is taught to understand the political institutions of our country, and to know how the country is vibrating with new emotions, with new aspirations, with a new life.

But we want also the steady light, the infallible light, of religious faith, not a faith which merely appeals to the intelligence, but a faith which is indelibly inscribed on the heart. First, we want to realize that religious consciousness, and immediately we have done that, I think the whole department of life is open to us, and it should then be a sacred privilege of students and everybody to partake of that whole life, so that, when they grow to manhood, and when they leave their colleges, they may do so as men properly equipped to battle with life.

Today what happens is this: much of the political life is confined to student life; immediately the students leave their colleges and cease to be students, they sink into oblivion, they seek miserable employments, carrying miserable emoluments, rising no higher in their aspirations, knowing nothing of God, knowing nothing of fresh air or bright light, and nothing of that real vigorous independence that comes out of obedience to these laws that I have ventured to place before you.

Conclusion

I am not here asking you to crowd into the ashram, there is no room there. But I say that every one of you may enact that ashram life individually and collectively. I shall be satisfied with anything that you may choose from the rules I have ventured to place before you and act up to it. But if you think that these are the outpourings of a mad man, you will not hesitate to tell me that it is so, and I shall take that judgment from you undismayed.

A History of the
Satyagraha Ashram

Gandhi commenced writing this unfinished history while in Yeravda Central Prison on April 5, 1932. He worked on it intermittently and wrote the last available installment on July 11, 1932.

Introduction

Ashram here means a community of men of religion. Looking at the past in the light of the present, I feel that an ashram was a necessary of life for me. As soon as I had a house of my own, my house was an ashram in this sense, for my life as a house-holder was not one of enjoyment but of duty discharged from day to day. Again, besides the members of my family, I always had some friends or others living with me whose relation with me was spiritual from the first or became such later on. This went on unconsciously till 1904 when I read Ruskin's *Unto This Last*, which made a deep impression on me. I determined to take *Indian Opinion* into a forest where I should live with the workers as members of my family.

I purchased one hundred acres of land and founded Phoenix Settlement, which neither we nor anyone else called an ashram. It had a religious basis, but the visible object was purity of body and mind as well as economic equality. I did not then consider *brahmacharya*, chastity, to be essential; on the other hand it was expected that co-workers would live as family men and have children. A brief account of Phoenix will be found in *Satyagraha in South Africa*.

This was the first step.

The second step was taken in 1906. I learnt in the school of experience that *brahmacharya* was a *sine qua non* for a life devoted to service. From this time onward I looked upon Phoenix deliberately as a religious institution. The same year witnessed the advent of satyagraha [truth-force, non-violent resistance], which was based on religion and implied an unshakable faith in the God of truth. Religion here should not be understood in a narrow sense, but as that which acts as a link between different religions and realizes their essential unity.

This went on till 1911. All these years the Phoenix Settlement was progressing as an ashram, though we did not call it by that name.

We took the third step in 1911. So far only those people lived at Phoenix who were working in the press and the paper. But now as a part of the satyagraha movement we felt the need of an ashram where satyagrahi families could live and lead a religious life. I had already come in contact with my German friend, Kallenbach. Both of us were living a sort of ashram life. I was a barrister and Kallenbach an architect. However we led a comparatively very simple life in the sparsely populated country, and were religiously minded. We might commit mistakes out of ignorance, but we were trying to seek the root of every activity in religion. Kallenbach purchased a farm of 1,100 acres and the satyagrahi families settled there.

Religious problems confronted us now at every step and the whole institution was managed from a religious standpoint. Among the settlers there were Hindus, Mussalmans, Christians and Parsis. But I do not remember that they ever quarreled with one another, though each was staunch in his own faith. We respected one another's religion and tried to help everybody to follow his own faith and thus to make spiritual progress. This institution was not known as Satyagraha Ashram but as Tolstoy Farm. Kallenbach and I were followers of Tolstoy and endeavored to practice much of his doctrine. Tolstoy Farm was closed in 1912, and the farmers were sent to Phoenix. The history of Tolstoy Farm will also be found in *Satyagraha in South Africa.*

Phoenix now was no longer meant for the workers of *Indian Opinion* only; it was a satyagraha institution. That was only to be expected, for *Indian Opinion* owed its very existence to satyagraha. Still it was a great change. The even tenor of the lives of the settlers at Phoenix was disturbed, and they had now to discern certainty in the midst of uncertainty like the satyagrahis. But they were equal to the new demands made upon them. As at Tolstoy Farm, so also at Phoenix, I established a common kitchen which some joined while others had private kitchens of their own. The congregational prayer in the evening played a large part in our lives. And the final satyagraha campaign was started by the inmates of Phoenix Settlement in 1913.

The struggle ended in 1914. I left South Africa in July that year. It was decided that all settlers who wanted to go to India should be enabled to go there. Before going to India I had to meet Gokhale in England. The idea was to found a new institution in India for those who went there from Phoenix. And the community life commenced in South Africa was to be continued in India. I reached India early in 1915 with a view to establish an ashram though I was still unaware that I would call it by that name.

I toured all parts of India for a year, and visited some institutions from which I had much to learn. I was invited by several cities to establish the ashram in their neighborhood with a promise of assistance in various ways. Ahmedabad was selected at last. This was the fourth, and I imagine the last step. Whether or not it will always be the last is something of which no forecast is possible. How was the new institution to be named? What should be its rules and regulations? On these points I had full discussions and correspondence with friends, as a result of which we decided to call the institution Satya-graha Ashram. It is an appropriate name if we take its object into consideration. My life is devoted to the quest of truth. I would live and, if need be, die in prosecuting it, and of course I would take with me as many fellow pilgrims as I could get.

The ashram was established in a rented house at Kochrab on May 25, 1915. Some citizens of Ahmedabad undertook to finance it. At the beginning there were about twenty inmates, most of them from South Africa. Of these again the large majority spoke Tamil or Telugu. The chief activity in the ashram at this time was teaching Sanskrit, Hindi and Tamil to the old as well as the young, who also received some general education. Handweaving was the principal industry, with some carpentry as accessory to it. No servants were engaged, therefore cooking, sanitation, fetching water—everything was attended to by the ashramites. Truth and other observances were obligatory on them all. Distinctions of caste were not observed. Untouchability had not only no place in the ashram, but its eradication from Hindu society was one of our principal objectives. Emancipation of women from some customary bonds was insisted upon from the first. Therefore women in the ashram enjoy full freedom. Then again it was an ashram rule that persons following a particular faith should have the same feeling for followers of other faiths as for their co-religionists.

But for one thing I was solely responsible, and I am indebted to the West for it. I refer to my dietetic experiments, which commenced in 1888 when I went to England for studies. I always invite members of my family and other co-workers to join in. The experiments were designed to achieve three objects:

1. To acquire control over the palate as a part of self-control in general;
2. to find out which diet was the simplest and the cheapest so that by adopting it we might identify ourselves with the poor; and
3. to discover which diet was necessary for perfect health, as maintenance of health is largely dependent upon correct diet.

If in England I had not been under a vow to be a vegetarian, I might perhaps never have undertaken experiments in diet. But once I began to experiment, these three objectives took me into deeper waters, and I was led to make various kinds of experiments. And the ashram too joined in, though these experiments were not a part of ashram discipline.

The reader has perhaps now seen that the ashram set out to remedy what it thought were defects in our national life from the religious, economic and political standpoints. As we gathered new experiences, we undertook fresh activities. Even now I cannot say that the ashram has embarked on all possible activities that I can think of. There have been two limitations. First, we were sure we must cut our coat according to our cloth, that is, we must manage with what funds were placed at our disposal by friends without any special effort in collection. Secondly, we should not go in search of new spheres of activity, but if any activity naturally suggested itself to our minds, we should go in for it without counting the cost.

These two limitations spring from a religious attitude. This implies faith in God, that is, doing everything in dependence upon, and under the inspiration of, God. The man of religion conducts such activities as are sent by God with such resources as God places at his disposal. God never lets us see that he himself does anything; he achieves his aims through men inspired by him. When help was received from unexpected quarters or from friends without our asking for it, my faith led me to believe that it was sent by God. Similarly when some activity came to us unsought so that not to take it up would have been sheer cowardice, laziness or the like, I thought it was a godsend.

The same principle applies to co-workers as to material resources and to activities. We may have the funds and know how they are to be used, but we can do nothing in the absence of co-workers. Co-workers also should come unsought. We did not merely imagine, but had a living faith, that the ashram was God's. If therefore he wished to make the ashram his instrument as regards any activity, it was for him to place the requisite men and munitions at the ashram's disposal. Phoenix, Tolstoy Farm and Sabarmati Ashram have all been conducted more or less according to these principles, consciously or unconsciously. Ashram rules were observed at first with some laxity, but the observance has become stricter from day to day.

The ashram population doubled itself in a few months. Again the Kochrab bungalow was a hardly suitable building for an ashram. It would do for one well-to-do family, but not for sixty men, women and children engaged in various activities and observing *brahmacharya* and other vows. However we had to manage with what building was available. But very soon it became impossible to live in it for a number of reasons. As if God wanted to drive us out of it, we had suddenly to go out in search of a new site and to vacate the bungalow. The curious will look up the *Autobiography* for an account of these events. There was one defect in the ashram at Kochrab which was remedied after we had removed to Sabarmati. An ashram without orchard, farm or cattle would not be a complete unit. At Sabarmati we had cultivable land and therefore went in for agriculture at once.

Such is the prehistory and history of the ashram. I now propose to deal with its observances and activities in so far as I remember them. My diary is not at hand. Even if it is, it takes no note of the personal history of the ashramites. I therefore depend upon memory alone. This is nothing new for me, as *Satyagraha in South Africa* and the *Autobiography* were written in tile same manner. The reader will please bear this limitation in mind, as he goes through these pages.

Truth

Whenever someone was found telling a lie in the ashram, effective steps were taken to deal with the situation as symptomatic of a serious disease. The ashram does not believe in punishing wrongdoers, so much so that hesitation is felt even in asking them to leave the institution. Three lines of preventive action were therefore adopted.

The first thing attended to was the purity of the principal workers in charge, the idea being that if they were free from fault, the atmosphere about them was bound to be affected by their innocence. Untruth cannot stand before truth like darkness before the light of the sun.

Secondly, we had recourse to confession. If someone was found practicing untruth, the fact was brought to the notice of the congregation. This is a very useful measure if it is judiciously adopted. But one has to be careful about two things. The public confession must not be tainted by even a trace of force; and the confession should not lead to the person confessing taking leave of all sense of shame. If he comes to believe that mere confession has washed off his sin, he is no longer ashamed of it at all. There should be an ever present consciousness of the fact that the least little untruth is a dangerous thing.

Thirdly, the worker in charge of the ashram as well as the wrongdoer would fast as a matter of penance. Of course it is a matter for the wrongdoer himself to decide whether or not he should undertake a fast. But as for the worker in charge, he is clearly responsible for intentional and unintentional wrongdoing in his institution. Untruth is more poisonous and more subtle than any poison gas whatever, but it dare not enter where the head of the institution is wide awake and has a spiritual outlook on life. Still, if it is found to have effected an entrance, it is a warning to the principal worker, who may be sure that he must bear his share of responsibility for this infection. I for one believe that spiritual acts have clearly defined results precisely like combinations or processes in the natural sciences. Only as we have no such means of measurement in the former case as in the latter, we are not ready to believe, or we only halfheartedly believe, in the spiritual influences. Again, we are inclined to be lenient to ourselves with the result that our experiments are unsuccessful and we tend to move only in a circle like the oil-miller's bullock. Thus untruth gets a long lease of life, and at last we reach the melancholy conclusion that it is unavoidable. And what is unavoidable easily becomes necessary, so that not truth, but untruth increases its own prestige.

When therefore untruth was discovered in the ashram, I readily pleaded guilty for it myself. That is to say, I have not still attained truth as defined by me. It may be due to ignorance, but it is clear that I have not fully understood truth, and therefore neither even thought it out nor declared it, still less practiced it. But granting all this, was I to leave the ashram, and resort to some Himalayan cave and impose silence upon myself? That would be sheer cowardice. The quest of truth cannot be prosecuted in a cave. Silence makes no sense where it is necessary to speak. One may live in a cave in certain circumstances, but the common man can be tested only in society.

What then is the remedy to be tried to get rid of untruth? The only answer which suggests itself to me is bodily penance, that is fasting and the like. Bodily penance has a threefold influence, first over the penitent, secondly over the wrongdoer and thirdly over the congregation. The penitent becomes more alert, examines the innermost recesses of his own heart and takes steps to deal with any personal weakness that he may discover. If the wrongdoer has any pity, he becomes conscious of his own fault, is ashamed of it, and resolves never to sin any more in the future. The congregation takes a course of self-introspection.

But bodily penance is only a means to an end, not an end in itself. By itself it cannot bring an erring person to the right path. It is profitable only if it is accompanied by a certain line of thinking, which is as follows:

Man tends to become a slave of his own body, and engages in many activities and commits many sins for the sake of physical enjoyment. He should therefore mortify the flesh whenever there is an occasion of sin. A man given to physical enjoyment is subject to delusion. Even a slight renunciation of enjoyment in the shape of food will probably be helpful in breaking the power of that delusion. Fasting in order to produce this effect must be taken in its widest sense as the exercise of control over all the organs of sense with a view to the purification of oneself or others. Merely giving up food does not amount to a fast. And fasting for health is no fasting at all in this sense.

I have also found that frequent fasting tends to rob it of its efficacy, for then it becomes almost a mechanical process without any background of thought. Every fast therefore should be undertaken after due deliberation.

I have noted one special effect of fasting in my own case. I have fasted frequently; therefore my co-workers are nervous and are afraid that a fresh fast may place my life in danger. This fear makes them observe certain rules. I consider this an undesirable consequence of fasting. I do not however think that self-control practiced on account of such fear does any harm. This fear is inspired by love, and therefore it is a good thing if a person steers clear of wrongdoing even under the influence of such fear.

One painful consequence of fasting must be taken into account. People sometimes do not avoid sin but only try to hide it for fear that someone else may fast if he comes to know of it.

I hold that penance is necessary in certain cases and it has benefited the ashram on the whole. But one who undertakes it must possess certain qualifications:

1. The wrongdoer should have love for the penitent. The penitent may have love for the wrongdoer; but if the wrongdoer is unaware of it or
adopts an inimical attitude towards the penitent,
penance for him is out of the question. As he
regards himself as an enemy of the penitent, he
hates the latter. There is therefore a possibility
of the fast affecting him in a manner contrary to
all expectations, or acting as brute force employed
against him and thus regarded by him as a form
of coercion. Moreover, if everyone is supposed
to be entitled to undertake penance for the fail-
ings of others who do not stand in a special relation to him, there would be no end to the program of penance. Penance for the sins of the
whole world might befit a mahatma (great soul),
but here we are concerned with the common man.

2. The penitent himself must be one of the parties
wronged. That is to say, one should not do penance for a failing with which he is not in any way
concerned. Thus, suppose A and B are friends. B
is a member of the ashram, but A has nothing to
do with it. B has wronged the ashram. Here A
has neither the duty nor the right to undertake a
penance for B's fault. His interference might even
complicate the situation both for the ashram and
B. He may not even possess the necessary material to pronounce a judgment on B's conduct. By
agreeing to B's admission to the ashram, A must

be regarded as having transferred to the ashram his responsibility for B's good conduct.

3. A penitent for another's wrongdoing must himself be guiltless of similar misconduct. "The pot may not call the kettle black."

4. The penitent must otherwise also be a man of purity and appear such to the wrongdoer. Penance for another's wrongdoing presupposes purity; and if the guilty man has no respect for the penitent, the latter's fast might easily have an unhealthy effect upon him.

5. The penitent must not have any personal interest to serve. Thus, if A has promised to pay B ten rupees, non-payment of it is a fault. But B may not perform penance for A's failure to redeem his promise.

6. The penitent must not have any anger in him. If a father commences a fast in anger for a fault of his son, that is not penance. There should be nothing but compassion in penance, the object being the purification of oneself as well as of the guilty person.

7. The wrong act must be patent, accepted as such by all and spiritually harmful, and the doer must be aware of its nature. There should be no penance for inferential guilt, as it might at times have dangerous consequences. There should be no room for doubt as regards the fault. Moreover, one should not do penance for an act which he alone regards as wrong. It is possible that what one holds to be wrong today he might regard as

innocent tomorrow. So the wrong must be one that is accepted as such by society. For instance, I might regard the non-wearing of khadi to be very wrong. But my co-worker might see nothing wrong in it, or might not attach much importance to it, and so might or might not wear it as he wishes. If I regard this as a wrong and fast for it, that is not penance but coercion. There can be no penance also where the wrongdoer is not conscious of having done anything wrong.

The discussion of this topic is necessary for an institution in which there is no place for punishment or which always strives to act in a religious spirit. In such institutions the penance on the part of the heads of the ashram takes the place of penal measures. It would be impossible to maintain its purity in any other way. Punishment and disciplinary action might make for an outer show of orderliness and progress, but that is all. On the other hand penance preserves the institution both internally and externally and makes the institution firmer day by day. Hence the necessity for some such rules as those given above.

Fasts and such other penance have been undertaken in the ashram. Still it is far, far indeed, from its ideal of truth, and therefore, as we shall see later on, we now call it by the name of Udyoga Mandir, Temple of Industry. But we can certainly say that the men in charge of the ashram are wide awake, fully conscious of their imperfections and constantly trying to make sure that untruth does not find a foothold anywhere. But in an institution to which new members are being admitted from time to time, and that too only on trust, and which is

frequented by men from all provinces of India and some foreign countries, it is no easy thing to keep all of them on the
strait and narrow path. But if only the men at the top are true
to themselves, the ashram is sure to stand the test, no matter
how hard it is. There is no limit to the potency of truth, as
there is a limit to the power of an individual seeker. But if he
is wide awake and is striving constantly, there is no limit to his
power as well.

Prayer

If insistence on truth constitutes the root of the ashram, prayer
is the principal feeder of that root. The social (as distinguished
from the individual) activities of the ashram commence every
day with the congregational morning worship at 4:15 to 4:45
A.M. and close with the evening prayer at 7 to 7.30 P.M. Ever
since the ashram was founded, not a single day has passed to
my knowledge without this worship. I know of several occasions when owing to the rains only one responsible person
was present on the prayer ground. All inmates are expected to
attend the worship except in the case of illness or similar com-
pelling reason for absence. This expectation has been fairly
well fulfilled at the evening prayer, but not in the morning.

The time for morning worship was as a matter of experiment fixed at 4, 5, 6 and 7 A.M., one after another. But on
account of my persistently strong attitude on the subject, it
has been fixed at last at 4:20 A.M. With the first bell at 4
everyone rises from bed and after a wash reaches the prayer
ground by 4:20.

I believe that in a country like India the sooner a man
rises from bed the better. Indeed millions must necessarily

rise early. If the peasant is a late riser, his crops will suffer damage. Cattle are attended to and cows are milked early in the morning. Such being the case, seekers of saving truth, servants of the people or monks may well be up at 2 or 3; it would be surprising if they are not. In all countries of the world devotees of God and tillers of the soil rise early. Devotees take the name of God and peasants work in their fields serving the world as well as themselves. To my mind both are worshippers. Devotees are deliberately such while cultivators by their industry worship God unawares, as it helps to sustain the world. If instead of working in the fields, they took to religious meditation, they would be failing in their duty and involving themselves and the world in ruin.

We may or may not look upon the cultivator as a devotee, but where peasants, laborers and other people have willy nilly to rise early, how can a worshipper of truth or servant of the people be a late riser? Again in the ashram we are trying to coordinate work and worship. Therefore I am definitely of opinion that all able-bodied people in the ashram must rise early even at the cost of inconvenience. Four A.M. is not early but the latest time when we must be up and doing.

Then again we had to take a decision on certain questions. Where should the prayers be offered? Should we erect a temple or meet in the open air? Then again, should we raise a platform or sit in the sands or the dust? Should there be any images? At last we decided to sit on the sands under the canopy of the sky and not to install any image. Poverty is an ashram observance. The ashram exists in order to serve the starving millions. The poor have a place in it no less than others. It receives with open arms all who are willing to keep the rules, In such an institution the house of worship cannot be built with bricks and mortar, the sky must suffice for roof and the quarters for walls and pillars. A platform was planned but discarded later on, as its size would depend upon the indeterminate number of worshippers. And a big one would cost a large sum of money. Experience has shown the soundness of the decision not to build a house or even a platform. People from outside also attend the ashram prayers, so that at times the multitude present cannot be accommodated on the biggest of platforms.

Again as the ashram prayers are being increasingly imitated elsewhere, the sky-roofed temple has proved its utility. Morning and evening prayers are held wherever I go. Then there is such large attendance, especially in the evening, that prayers are possible only on open grounds. And if I had been in the habit of worshipping in a prayer hall only, I might perhaps never have thought of public prayers during my tours.

Then again all religions are accorded equal respect in the ashram. Followers of all faiths are welcome there; they may or may not believe in the worship of images. No image is kept at the congregational worship of the ashram in order to avoid hurting anybody's feelings. But if an ashramite wishes to keep an image in his room, he is free to do so.

At the morning prayer we first recite the *shlokas* (verses) printed in *Ashram Bhajanavali* (hymnal), and then sing one *bhajan* (hymn) followed by *Ramdhun* (repetition of Ramanama) and *Gitapath* (recitation of the *Gita*). In the evening we have recitation of the last nineteen verses of the second chapter of the *Gita*, one *bhajan* and *Ramdhun*, and then read some portion of a sacred book.

The *shlokas* were selected by Shri Kaka Kalelkar who has

been in the ashram since its foundation. Shri Maganlal Gandhi met him in Santiniketan [the ashram of poet Rabindranath Tagore], when he and the children of the Phoenix Settlement went there from South Africa while I was still in England. Dinabandhu Andrews and the late Mr. Pearson were then in Santiniketan. I had advised Maganlal to stay at some place selected by Andrews. And Andrews selected Santiniketan for the party. Kaka was a teacher there and came into close contact with Maganlal. Maganlal had been feeling the want of a Sanskrit teacher which was supplied by Kaka. Chintamani Shastri assisted him in the work. Kaka taught the children how to recite the verses repeated in prayer. Some of these verses were omitted in the ashram prayer in order to save time. Such is the history of the verses recited at the morning prayer all these days.

The recitation of these verses has often been objected to on the ground of saving time or because it appeared to some people that they could not well be recited by a worshipper of truth or by a non-Hindu. There is no doubt that these verses are recited only in Hindu society, but I cannot see why a non-Hindu may not join in or be present at the recitation. Muslim and Christian friends who have heard the verses have not raised any objection. Indeed they need not cause annoyance to anyone who respects other faiths as much as he respects his own. They do not contain any reflection on other people. Hindus being in an overwhelming majority in the ashram, the verses must be selected from the sacred books of the Hindus. Not that nothing is sung or recited from non-Hindu scriptures. Indeed there were occasions on which Imam Saheb recited verses from the Koran. Muslim and Christian hymns are often sung.

But the verses were strongly attacked from the standpoint of truth. An ashramite modestly but firmly argued that the worship of Sarasvati, Ganesh and the like was violence done to truth; for no such divinities really existed as Sarasvati seated on a lotus with a *vina* (kind of musical instrument) in her hands, or as Ganesh with a big belly and an elephant's trunk. To this argument I replied as follows:

"I claim to be a votary of truth, and yet I do not mind reciting these verses or teaching them to the children. If we condemn some *shlokas* on the strength of this argument, it would be tantamount to an attack on the very basis of Hinduism. Not that we may not condemn anything in Hinduism which is fit for condemnation, no matter how ancient it is. But I do not believe that this is a weak or vulnerable point of Hinduism. On the other hand I hold that it is perhaps characteristic of our faith. Sarasvati and Ganesh are not independent entities. They are all descriptive names of one God. Devoted poets have given a local habitation and a name to His countless attributes. They have done nothing wrong. Such verses deceive neither the worshippers nor others. When a human being praises God he imagines Him to be such as he thinks fit. The God of his imagination is there for him. Even when we pray to a God devoid of form and attributes we do in fact endow Him with attributes. And attributes too are form. Fundamentally God is indescribable in words. We mortals must of necessity depend upon the imagination which makes and sometimes mars us too. The qualities we attribute to God with the purest of motives are true for us but fundamentally false, because all attempts at describing Him must be unsuccessful. I am intellectually conscious of this and still I cannot help dwelling upon the attributes of God. My intellect can exercise no influence over my heart. I am prepared to admit that my heart in its weakness hankers after a God with attributes. The *shlokas* which I have been reciting every day for the last fifteen years give me peace and hold good for me. In them I find beauty as well as poetry. Learned men tell many stories about Sarasvati, Ganesh and the like, which have their own use. I do not know their deeper meaning, as I have not gone into it, finding it unnecessary for me. It may be that my ignorance is my salvation. I did not see that I needed to go deep into this as a part of my quest of truth. It is enough that I know my God, and although I have still to realize His living presence, I am on the right path to my destination."

I could hardly expect that the objectors should be satisfied with this reply. An *ad hoc* committee examined the whole question fully and finally recommended that the *shlokas* should remain as they were, for every possible selection would be viewed with disfavor by someone or other.

A hymn was sung after the *shlokas*. Indeed singing hymns was the only item of the prayers in South Africa. The *shlokas* were added in India. Maganlal Gandhi was our leader in song. But we felt that the arrangement was unsatisfactory. We should have an expert singer for the purpose, and that singer should be one who would observe the ashram rules. One such was found in Narayan Moreshwar Khare, a pupil of Pandit Vishnu Digambar, whom the master kindly sent to the ashram. Pandit Khare gave us full satisfaction and is now a full member of the ashram. He made hymn singing interesting, and the *Ashram Bhajanavali* (hymnal) which is now read by thousands was in the main compiled by him. He introduced *Ramdhun*, the third item of our prayers.

The fourth item is recitation of verses from the *Gita*. The *Gita* has for years been an authoritative guide to belief and conduct for the Satyagraha Ashram. It has provided us with a test with which to determine the correctness or otherwise of ideas and courses of conduct in question. Therefore we wished that all ashramites should understand the meaning of the *Gita* and if possible commit it to memory. If this last was not possible, we wished that they should at least read the original Sanskrit with correct pronunciation. With this end in view we began to recite part of the *Gita* every day. We would recite a few verses every day and continue the recitation until we had learnt them by heart.

The recitation is now so arranged that the whole of the *Gita* is finished in fourteen days, and everybody knows what verses will be recited on any particular day. The first chapter is recited on every alternate Friday, and we shall come to it on Friday next (June 10, 1932). The seventh and eighth, the twelfth and thirteenth, the fourteenth and fifteenth, and the sixteenth and seventeenth chapters are recited on the same day in order to finish eighteen chapters in fourteen days.

At the evening prayer we recite the last nineteen verses of the second chapter of the *Gita* as well as sing a hymn and re-peat Ramanama. These verses describe the characteristics of the *sthitaprajna* (the man of stable understanding), which a satyagrahi too must acquire, and are recited in order that he may constantly bear them in mind.

Repeating the same thing at prayer from day to day is objected to on the ground that it thus becomes mechanical and tends to be ineffective. It is true that the prayer becomes mechanical. We ourselves are machines, and if we believe God to be our mover, we must behave like machines in His hands.

If the sun and other heavenly bodies did not work like machines, the universe would come to a standstill. But in behaving like machines, we must not behave like inert matter. We are intelligent beings and must observe rules as such.

The point is not whether the contents of the prayer are always the same or differ from day to day. Even if they are full of variety, it is possible that they will become ineffective. The Gayatri verse among Hindus, the confession of faith, *kalma*, among Mussalmans, the typical Christian prayer in the Sermon on the Mount, have been recited by millions for centuries every day; and yet their power has not diminished but is ever on the increase. It all depends upon the spirit behind the recitation. If an unbeliever or a parrot repeats these potent words, they will fall quite flat. On the other hand when a believer utters them always, their influence grows from day to day. Our staple food is the same. The wheat eater will take other things besides wheat, and these additional things may differ from time to time, but the wheat bread will always be there on the dining table. It is the eater's staff of life, and he will never weary of it. If he conceives a dislike for it, that is a sign of the approaching dissolution of his body.

The same is the case with prayer. Its principal contents must be always the same. If the soul hungers after them, she will not quarrel with the monotony of the prayer but will derive nourishment from it. She will have a sense of deprivation on the day that it has not been possible to offer prayer. She will be more downcast than one who observes a physical fast. Giving up food may now and then be beneficial for the body; indigestion of prayer for the soul is something never heard of.

The fact is that many of us offer prayer without our soul

being hungry for it. It is a fashion to believe that there is a soul; so we believe that she exists. Such is the sorry plight of many among us. Some are intellectually convinced that there is a soul, but they have not grasped that truth with the heart; therefore they do not feel the need for prayer. Many offer prayer because they live in society and think they must participate in its activities. No wonder they hanker after variety. As a matter of fact however they do not *attend* prayer. They want to enjoy the music or are merely curious or wish to listen to the sermon. They are not there to be one with God.

Prarthana (Gujarati word for prayer) literally means to ask for something, that is, to ask God for something in a spirit of humility. Here it is not used in that sense, but in the sense of praising or worshipping God, meditation and self-purification.

But who is God? God is not some person outside ourselves or away from the universe. He pervades everything, and is omniscient as well as omnipotent. He does not need any praise or petitions. Being immanent in all beings, He hears everything and reads our innermost thoughts. He abides in our hearts and is nearer to us than the nails are to the fingers. What is the use of telling Him anything?

It is in view of this difficulty that *prarthana* is further paraphrased as self-purification. When we speak out aloud at prayer time, our speech is addressed not to God but to ourselves, and is intended to shake off our torpor. Some of us are intellectually aware of God, while others are afflicted by doubt. None has seen Him face to face. We desire to recognize and realize Him, to become one with Him, and seek to gratify that desire through prayer.

———

This God whom we seek to realize is truth. Or to put it in another way truth is God. This truth is not merely the truth we are expected to speak. It is That which alone is, which constitutes the stuff of which all things are made, which subsists by virtue of its own power, which is not supported by anything else but supports everything that exists. Truth alone is eternal, everything else is momentary. It need not assume shape or form. It is pure intelligence as well as pure bliss. We call It Ishvara because everything is regulated by Its will. It and the law It promulgates are one. Therefore it is not a blind law. It governs the entire universe. To propitiate this truth is *prarthana,* which in effect means an earnest desire to be filled with the spirit of truth. This desire should be present all the twenty-four hours. But our souls are too dull to have this awareness day and night. Therefore we offer prayers for a short time in the hope that a time will come when all our conduct will be one continuously sustained prayer.

Such is the ideal of prayer for the ashram, which at present is far, far away from it. The detailed program outlined above is something external, but the idea is to make our very hearts prayerful. If the ashram prayers are not still attractive, if even the inmates of the ashram attend them under compulsion of a sort, it only means that none of us is still a man of prayer in the real sense of the term.

In heartfelt prayer the worshipper's attention is concentrated on the object of worship so much so that he is not conscious of anything else besides. The worshipper has well been compared to a lover. The lover forgets the whole world and even himself in the presence of the beloved. The identification of the worshipper with God should be closer still. It comes only after much striving, self-suffering, *tapas* [self-control], and self-discipline. In a place which such a worshipper sanctifies by his presence, no inducements need be offered to people for attending prayers, as they are drawn to the house of prayer by the force of his devotion.

We have dealt so far with congregational prayer, but great stress is also laid in the ashram on individual and solitary prayer. One who never prays by himself may attend congregational prayers but will not derive much advantage from them. They are absolutely necessary for a congregation, but as a congregation is made up of individuals, they are fruitless without individual prayers. Every member of the ashram is therefore reminded now and then that he should of his own accord give himself up to self-introspection at all times of the day. No watch can be kept that he does this, and no account can be maintained of such silent prayer. I cannot say how far it prevails in the ashram, but I believe that some are making more or less effort in that direction.

Ahimsa

The greatest difficulties perhaps were encountered as regards the observance of ahimsa. There are problems of truth, but it is not very hard to understand what truth is. But in understanding ahimsa we every now and then find ourselves out of our depth. Ahimsa was discussed in the ashram at greater length than any other subject. Even now the question often arises whether a particular act is violent or non-violent. And even if we know the distinction between violence and non-violence, we are often unable to satisfy the demand of nonviolence on account of weakness which cannot easily be overcome.

Ahimsa means not to hurt any living creature by thought,

word or deed, even for the supposed benefit of that creature. To observe this principle fully is impossible for men, who kill a number of living beings large and small as they breathe or blink or till the land. We catch and hurt snakes or scorpions for fear of being bitten and leave them in some out-of-the-way place if we do not kill them. Hurting them in this way may be unavoidable, but is clearly *himsa* as defined above.

If I save the food I eat or the clothes I wear or the space I occupy, it is obvious that these can be utilized by someone else whose need is greater than mine. As my selfishness prevents him from using these things, my physical enjoyment involves violence to my poorer neighbor. When I eat cereals and vegetables in order to support life, that means violence done to vegetable life.

Surrounded thus as I am by violence on all sides, how am I to observe nonviolence? Fresh difficulties are bound to arise at every step as I try to do so.

The violence described above is easily recognized as such. But what about our being angry with one another? A teacher inflicting corporal punishment on his pupils, a mother taking her children to task, a man losing his temper in his intercourse with equals, all these are guilty of violence, and violence of a bad type, which is not easy to tackle. Violence is there where there is attachment on the one hand and dislike on the other. How are we to get rid of it?

The first lesson therefore that we in the ashram must learn is that although to sever some person's head from his body for the sake of the country or the family or oneself is indeed a violent act, the subtle violence involved in injuring the feelings of other people day in and day out is possibly very much worse than that. Murders committed in the world will seem to be numerous when considered by themselves and not so numerous when compared with the number of deaths due to other causes; but the subtle violence involved in daily loss of temper and the like defies all attempts at calculation.

We are constantly striving in the ashram to deal with all these kinds of violence. All of us realize our own weakness. All of us including myself are afraid of snakes, for instance. We therefore as a rule catch them and put them out of harm's way. But if someone kills a snake out of fear, he is not taken to task. There was once a snake in the cowshed, and it was impossible to catch it where it was. It was a risky thing to keep the cattle there; the men also were afraid of working thereabouts. Maganlal Gandhi felt helpless and permitted them to kill that snake. I approved of his action when he told me about it. I believe that even if I had been there on the spot, I could not have done anything other than what he did. My intellect tells me that I must treat even a snake as my kinsman and at the risk of losing my life I must hold the snake in my hands and take it away from those who are afraid of it. But in my heart I do not harbor the necessary love, fearlessness and readiness to die of snake-bite. I am trying to cultivate all these qualities but have not still succeeded in the attempt. It is possible that if I am attacked by a snake, I may neither resist nor kill it. But I am not willing to place anyone else's life in danger.

Once in the ashram the monkeys made a terrible nuisance of themselves and did extensive damage to the crops. The watchman tried to frighten them by making a show of hurling stones from a sling but in vain. He then actually threw stones and injured and crippled one of the monkeys. I thought this even worse than killing it. I therefore held discussions

with co-workers in the ashram, and finally we took the decision that if we could not get rid of the monkeys by gentle
means short of wounding them, we must kill one or two of
them and end the nuisance. Before this decision was taken
there was a public discussion in the columns of *Navajivan* which
may be consulted by the curious.

No one outside India thinks that one should not kill
even a violent animal. Some individuals like St. Francis observed this rule, but the common people did not, so far as I
am aware. The ashram believes in the principle, but it is a pity
that we have not succeeded in putting it into practice. We have
not still acquired the art of doing this. It is possible that many
men will have to lay down their lives before this art is mastered. For the present it is only a consummation devoutly to
be wished for. The principle has long been accepted in India
but the practice is very imperfect on account of our laziness
and self-deception.

Mad dogs are killed in the ashram, the idea being that
they die after much suffering and never recover. Our people
torture mad dogs instead of killing them and deceive themselves into thinking that they observe nonviolence. As a matter of fact they only indulge in greater violence.

Nonviolence sometimes calls upon us to put an end to
the life of a living being. For instance a calf in the ashram
dairy was lame and had developed terrible sores; it could not
eat and breathed with difficulty. After three days' argument
with myself and my co-workers, I had poison injected into its
body and thus put an end to its life. That action was nonviolent, because it was wholly unselfish inasmuch as the sole purpose was to achieve the calf's relief from pain. It was a surgical
operation, and I should do exactly the same thing with my

child, if he were in the same predicament.

Many Hindus were shocked at this, but their reaction to the incident only betrays their ignorance of the nature of ahimsa, which has for us long ceased to be a living faith, and has been degraded into formalities complied with when not very inconvenient.

Here we must take leave of the ashram experiments with ahimsa as regards sub-human species.

Ahimsa as regards sub-human life is from the ashram point of view an important aspect but still only one aspect of this comprehensive principle. Our dealings with our fellow men are still more important than that. The commonest form of human intercourse is either violent or nonviolent. Fortunately for humanity nonviolence pervades human life and is observed by men without special effort. If we had not borne with one another, mankind would have been destroyed long ago. Ahimsa would thus appear to be the law of life, but we are not thus far entitled to any credit for observing it.

Whenever there is a clash of ephemeral interests, men tend to resort to violence. But with a deliberate observance of nonviolence a person experiences a second birth or "conversion." We in the ashram are out to observe ahimsa intelligently. In so doing we meet with numerous obstacles, disappointments and trials of faith. We may not be satisfied with observing ahimsa in deed only. Not to think badly of anyone, not to wish ill to him though we have suffered at his hands, not to hurt him even in thought, this is an uphill task, but therein lies the acid test of our ahimsa.

Thieves have visited the ashram from outside, and there have been thieves in the ashram itself. But we do not believe in inflicting punishment on them. We do not inform the police;

we put up with the losses as best we may. This rule has been infringed at times. A thief was once caught red-handed by day. The ashramite who caught him bound him with a rope and treated him contemptuously. I was in the ashram at the time. I went to the thief, rebuked him and set him free. But as a matter of fact ahimsa demands from us something more than this. We must find out and apply methods which would put a stop to thieving altogether. For one thing we must diminish the number of our "possessions" so as not to tempt others. Secondly we must bring about a reformation in the surrounding villages. And thirdly the ashram ministry should be extended in scope so that the bad as well as the good would learn to look upon the settlement as their own.

We thus find that it is impossible for a man with "possessions" to observe ahimsa even in the gross meaning of that term. A man of property must adopt measures for its security involving the punishment of whoever tries to steal it. Only he can observe ahimsa who holds nothing as his own and works away in a spirit of total detachment. If there are many such individuals and organizations in society, violence will not be much in evidence. As gunpowder has a large place in a society based on violence and a soldier who can handle it with skill becomes entitled to honor and rewards, even so in a nonviolent society self-suffering and self-control are its "munitions of war," and persons endowed with these qualities are its natural protectors. The world at large has not still accepted ahimsa in this sense. India has accepted it more or less but not in a comprehensive manner. The ashram holds that ahimsa should be universal in scope, and that society can be built up on the foundations of ahimsa. It conducts experiments with this end in view, but these have not been very successful. I have been unable to cite in this chapter much that would hearten the votary of ahimsa. This does not apply of course to ahimsa as applied to politics, to which I propose to devote a separate chapter [This chapter was not written.].

Brahmacharya, or Chastity

This observance does not give rise to ever so many problems and dilemmas as ahimsa does. Its meaning is generally well understood; but understanding it is one thing, practicing it is quite another thing and calls forth all our powers. Many of us put forth a great effort but without making any progress. Some of us even lost ground previously won. None has reached perfection. But everyone realizes its supreme importance. My striving in this direction began before 1906 when I took the vow. There were many ups and downs. It was only after I had burnt my fingers at times that I realized the deeper meaning of brahmacharya. And then I found that expositions made in books cannot be understood without actual experience, and wear a fresh aspect in the light of it. Even in the case of a simple machine like the spinning wheel, it is one thing to read the directions for plying it, and it is another thing to put the directions into practice. New light dawns upon us as soon as we commence our practice. And what is true of simple tangible things like the wheel is still more true of spiritual states.

A brahmachari is one who controls his organs of sense in thought, word and deed. The meaning of this definition became somewhat clear after I had kept the observance for some time, but it is not quite clear even now, for I do not claim to be a perfect brahmachari, evil thoughts having been held in restraint but not eradicated. When they are eradicated, I will discover further implications of the definition.

Ordinary brahmacharya is not so difficult as it is supposed to be. We have made it difficult by understanding the
term in a narrow sense. Many of us play with brahmacharya
like fools who put their hands in the fire and still expect to
escape being burnt. Very few realize that a brahmachari has to
control not one but all the organs of sense. He is no
brahmachari who thinks that mere control of animal passion
is the be-all and end-all of brahmacharya. No wonder if he
finds it very difficult. He who attempts to control only one
organ and allows all the others free play must not expect to
achieve success. He might as well deliberately descend into a
well and expect to keep his body dry. Those who would achieve
an easy conquest of animal passion must give up all unnecessary things which stimulate it. They must control their palate
and cease to read suggestive literature and to enjoy all luxu-
ries. I have not the shadow of a doubt that they will find brahmacharya easy enough after such renunciation.

Some people think that it is not a breach of brahmacharya to cast a lascivious look at one's own or another's wife or to
touch her in the same manner; but nothing could be farther
from the truth. Such behavior constitutes a direct breach of
brahmacharya in the grosser sense of the term. Men and women
who indulge in it deceive themselves and the world, and grow-
ing weaker day by day, make themselves easily susceptible to
disease. If they stop short of a full satisfaction of desire, the
credit for it is due to circumstances and not to themselves.
They are bound to fall at the very first opportunity.

In brahmacharya as conceived by the ashram those who
are married behave as if they were not married. Married people
do well to renounce gratification outside the marital bond;

theirs is a limited brahmacharya. But to look upon them as brahmacharis is to do violence to that glorious term.

Such is the complete ashram definition of brahmacharya. However there are men as well as women in the ashram who enjoy considerable freedom in meeting one another. The ideal is that one ashramite should have the same freedom in meeting another as is enjoyed by a son in meeting his mother or by a brother in meeting his sister. That is to say, the restrictions that are generally imposed for the protection of brahmacharya are lifted in the Satyagraha Ashram, where we believe that brahmacharya which ever stands in need of such adventitious support is no brahmacharya at all. The restrictions may be necessary at first but must wither away in time. Their disappearance does not mean that a brahmachari goes about seeking the company of women, but it does mean that if there is an occasion for him to minister to a woman, he may not refuse such ministry under the impression that it is forbidden to him.

Woman for a brahmachari is not the "doorkeeper of hell" but is an incarnation of our Mother who is in Heaven. He is no brahmachari at all whose mind is disturbed if he happens to see a woman or if he has to touch her in order to render service. A brahmachari's reaction to a living image and to a bronze statue is one and the same. But a man who is perturbed at the very mention of woman and who is desirous of observing brahmacharya, must fly even from a figurine made of metal.

An ashram, where men and women thus live and work together, serve one another and try to observe brahmacharya, is exposed to many perils. Its arrangements involve to a certain extent a deliberate imitation of life in the West. I have grave doubts about my competence to undertake such an experiment. But this applies to all my experiments. It is on account of these doubts that I do not look upon anyone else as my disciple. Those who have joined the ashram after due deliberation have joined me as coworkers, fully conscious of all the risks involved therein. As for the young boys and girls, I look upon them as my own children, and as such they are automatically drawn within the pale of my experiments. These experiments are undertaken in the name of the God of truth. He is the master potter while we are mere clay in His hands.

My experience of the ashram so far has taught me that there is no ground for disappointment as regards the results of this pursuit of brahmacharya under difficulties. Men as well as women have on the whole derived benefit from it, but the greatest benefit has in my opinion accrued to women. Some of us have fallen, some have risen after sustaining fall. The possibility of stumbling is implicit in all such experimentation. Where there is cent per cent success, it is not an experiment but a characteristic of omniscience.

I now come to a point of vital importance which I have reserved for treatment towards the end of the discussion. We are told in the *Bhagavad Gita* (II.59) that "when a man starves his senses, the objects of those senses disappear from him, but not the yearning for them; the yearning too departs when he beholds the Supreme," that is to say, the truth or Brahman (God). The whole truth of the matter has here been set forth by the experienced Krishna. Fasting and all other forms of discipline are ineffective without the grace of God. What is the vision of the truth or God? It does not mean seeing something with the physical eye or witnessing a miracle. Seeing God means realization of the fact that God abides in one's heart. The yearning must persist until one has attained this realization, and will vanish upon realization. It is with this end in view that we keep observances, and engage ourselves in spiritual endeavor at the ashram. Realization is the final fruit of constant effort. The human lover sacrifices his all for his beloved, but his sacrifice is fruitless inasmuch as it is offered for the sake of momentary pleasure. But the quest of truth calls for even greater concentration than that of the human beloved. There is joy ineffable in store for the aspirant at the end of the quest. Still very few of us are as earnest as even the human lover. Such being the facts of the case, what is the use of complaining that the quest of truth is an uphill task? The human beloved may be at a distance of several thousand miles; God is there in the tabernacle of the human heart, nearer to us than the finger nails are to the fingers. But what is to be done with a man who wanders all over the wide world in search of treasure which as a matter of fact is buried under his very feet?

The brahmacharya observed by a self-restraining person is not something to be despised. It certainly serves to weaken the force of the yearning for the "flesh-pots of Egypt." One may keep fasts or adopt various other methods of mortifying the flesh, but the objects of sense must be compelled to disappear. The yearning will get itself in readiness to go as this process is on. Then the seeker will have the beatific vision, and that will be the signal for the yearning to make its final exit. The treasure supposed to be lost will be recovered. He who has not put all his strength into his effort has no right to complain that he has not "seen" Brahman. Observing brahmacharya is one of the means to the end which is seeing Brahman. Without brahmacharya no one may expect to see Him, and without seeing Him one cannot observe brahmacharya to perfection. The verse therefore does not rule out self-discipline but only indicates its limitations.

All members of the ashram, young as well as old, married as well as unmarried, try to observe brahmacharya, but only a few will observe it for life. When the young people come to years of discretion, they are told that they are not bound to observe brahmacharya any longer against their will, and that whoever feels that he is unable to put forth the requisite effort has a right to marry. And when he makes the request the ashram helps him in finding out a suitable partner in life. This position is very well understood, and the results have been uniformly good. The young men have persisted in larger numbers. The girls too have done pretty well. None of them married before she was fifteen, and many married only after they were nineteen.

Those who wish to marry with ashram assistance must rest satisfied with the simplest of religious ceremonies. There are no dinners, no guests invited from outside, no beating of drums. Both bride and bridegroom are dressed in hand-spun and hand-woven khadi. There are no ornaments in gold or silver. There is no marriage settlement and no dowry except a few clothes and a spinning-wheel. The function hardly costs even ten rupees, and takes not more than one hour. The bride and bridegroom recite in their own language the *mantras* (Vedic verses) of the *saptapadi* the purport of which has already been explained to them. On the day fixed for the marriage, the bride and bridegroom keep a fast, water trees, clean the cowshed and the ashram well and read the *Gita* before the ceremony. Those who give away the bride also fast until they have made the gift. We now insist that the ashram will not help to arrange a marriage between members of the same subcaste, and everyone is encouraged to seek his mate outside his own subcaste.

Non-Stealing and Non-Possession or Poverty

These two, along with truth, ahimsa and brahmacharya that have gone before, constitute the five *mahavratas* (primary observances) of old and have been included in the ashram observances as they are necessary for one who seeks self-realization. But they do not call for any lengthy discussion.

I. Non-Stealing

To take something from another without his permission is theft of course. But it is also theft to use a thing for a purpose different from the one intended by the lender or to use it for a period longer than that which has been fixed with him. The profound truth upon which this observance is based is that God never creates more than what is strictly needed for the moment. Therefore whoever appropriates more than the minimum that is really necessary for him is guilty of theft.

2. Non-Possession or Poverty

This is covered by Non-stealing. We may neither take nor keep a superfluous thing. It is therefore a breach of this observance to possess food or furniture which we do not really need. He who can do without chairs will not keep them in his house. The seeker will deliberately and voluntarily reduce his wants and cultivate progressively simple habits.

Non-stealing and Non-possession are mental states only. No human being can keep these observances to perfection. The body too is a possession, and so long as it is there, it calls for other possessions in its train. But the seeker will cultivate

the spirit of detachment and give up one possession after another. Everyone cannot be judged by the same standard. An
ant may fall from grace if it stores two grains instead of one.
An elephant on the other hand will have a lot of grass heaped
before itself and yet it cannot be charged with having "great
possessions."

These difficulties appear to have given rise to the current
conception of sannyasa (renunciation of the world), which is
not accepted by the ashram. Such sannyasa may be necessary
for some rare spirit who has the power of conferring benefits
upon the world by only thinking good thoughts in a cave. But
the world would be ruined if everyone became a cave-dweller.
Ordinary men and women can only cultivate mental detachment. Whoever lives in the world and lives in it only for serving it is a sannyasi.

We of the ashram hope to become sannyasis in this sense.
We may keep necessary things but should be ready to give up
everything including our bodies. The loss of nothing whatever
should worry us at all. So long as we are alive, we should render such service as we are capable of. It is a good thing if we
get food to eat and clothes to wear; it is also a good thing if we
don't. We should so train our minds that no ashramite will fail
to give a good account of himself when testing time comes.

Bread Labor

The ashram holds that every man and woman must work in
order to live. This principle came home to me upon reading
one of Tolstoy's essays. Referring to the Russian writer
Bondareff, Tolstoy observes that his discovery of the vital importance of bread labor is one of the most remarkable discov-

eries of modern times. The idea is that every healthy individual must labor enough for his food, and his intellectual faculties must be exercised not in order to obtain a living or amass a fortune but only in the service of mankind. If this principle is observed everywhere, all men would be equal, none would starve and the world would be saved from many a sin.

It is possible that this golden rule will never be observed by the whole world. Millions observe it in spite of themselves without understanding it. But their mind is working in a contrary direction, so that they are unhappy themselves and their labor is not as fruitful as it should be. This state of things serves as an incentive to those who understand and seek to practice the rule. By rendering a willing obedience to it they enjoy good health as well as perfect peace and develop their capacity for service.

Tolstoy made a deep impression on my mind, and even in South Africa I began to observe the rule to the best of my ability. And ever since the ashram was founded, bread labor has been perhaps its most characteristic feature.

In my opinion the same principle has been set forth in the third chapter of the *Gita*. I do not go so far as to say that the word *yajna* (sacrifice) there means body labor. But when the *Gita* says that "rain comes from sacrifice" (verse 14) , I think it indicates the necessity of bodily labor. The "residue of sacrifice" (verse 13) is the bread that we have won in the sweat of our brow. Laboring enough for one's food has been classed in the *Gita* as a *yajna*. Whoever eats more than is enough for sustaining the body is a thief, for most of us hardly perform labor enough to maintain themselves. I believe that a man has no right to receive anything more than his keep, and that everyone who labors is entitled to a living wage.

This does not rule out the division of labor. The manufacture of everything needed to satisfy essential human wants involves bodily labor, so that labor in all essential occupations counts as bread labor. But as many of us do not perform such labor, they have to take exercise in order to preserve their health. A cultivator working on his farm from day to day has not to take breathing exercise or stretch his muscles. Indeed if he observes the other laws of health, he will never be afflicted with illness.

God never creates more than what is strictly needed for the moment, with the result that if anyone appropriates more than he really needs, he reduces his neighbor to destitution. The starvation of people in several parts of the world is due to many of us seizing very much more than we need. We may utilize the gifts of nature just as we choose, but in her books the debits are always equal to the credits. There is no balance in either column.

This law is not invalidated by the fact that men raise bigger crops by mechanizing agriculture and using artificial fertilizers, and similarly increase the industrial output. This only means a transformation of natural energy. Try as we might, the balance is always nil.

Be that as it may, the observance best kept in the ashram is that of bread labor, and no wonder. Its fulfillment is easy with ordinary care. For certain hours in the day, there is nothing to be done but work. Work is therefore bound to be put in. A worker may be lazy, inefficient or inattentive, but he works for a number of hours all the same. Again certain kinds of labor are capable of yielding an immediate product and the worker cannot idle away a considerable amount of his time. In an institution where body labor plays a prominent part there are few servants. Drawing water, splitting firewood, cleaning and filling lamps with oil, sanitary service, sweeping the roads and houses, washing one's clothes, cooking—all these tasks must always be performed.

Besides this there are various activities carried on in the ashram as a result of and in order to help fulfillment of the observances, such as agriculture, dairying, weaving, carpentry, tanning and the like, which must be attended to by many members of the ashram.

All these activities may be deemed sufficient for keeping the observance of bread labor, but another essential feature of *yajna* (sacrifice) is the idea of serving others, and the ashram will perhaps be found wanting from this latter standpoint. The ashram ideal is to live to serve. In such an institution there is no room for idleness or shirking duty, and everything should be done with right goodwill. If this were actually the case, the ashram ministry would be more fruitful than it is. But we are still very far from such a happy condition. Therefore although in a sense every activity in the ashram is of the nature *of yajna,* it is compulsory for all to spin for at least one hour in the name of God incarnated as the Poor *(Daridranarayana).*

People often say that in an institution like the ashram where body labor is given pride of place there is no scope for intellectual development, but my experience is just the reverse. Everyone who has been to the ashram has made intellectual progress as well; I know of none who was the worse on account of a sojourn in the ashram.

Intellectual development is often supposed to mean a knowledge of facts concerning the universe. I freely admit that such knowledge is not laboriously imparted to the students in the ashram. But if intellectual progress spells understanding and discrimination, there is adequate provision for it in the ashram. Where body labor is performed for mere wages, it is possible that the laborer becomes dull and listless. No one tells him how and why things are done; he himself has no curiosity and takes no interest in his work. But such is not the case in the ashram. Everything including sanitary service must be done intelligently, enthusiastically and for the love of God. Thus there is scope for intellectual development in all departments of ashram activity. Everyone is encouraged to acquire full knowledge of his own subject. Anyone who neglects to do this must answer for it. Everyone in the ashram is a laborer; none is a wage-slave.

It is a gross superstition to imagine that knowledge is acquired only through books. We must discard this error. Reading books has a place in life, but is useful only in its own place. If book knowledge is cultivated at the cost of body labor, we must raise a revolt against it. Most of our time must be devoted to body labor, and only a little to reading. As in India today the rich and the so-called higher classes despise body labor, it is very necessary to insist on the dignity of labor. Even for real intellectual development one should engage in some useful bodily activity.

It is desirable if at all possible that the ashram should give the workers some more time for reading. It is also desirable that illiterate ashramites should have a teacher to help them in their studies. But it appears that time for reading and the like cannot be given at the cost of any of the present activities of the ashram. Nor can we engage paid teachers, and so long as the ashram cannot attract more men who are capable of teaching ordinary school subjects, we have to manage with as many such as we have got in our midst. The school and college-educated men who are in the ashram have not still fully acquired the skill of correlating the three R's with body labor. This is a new experiment for all of us. But we shall learn from experience, and those of us who have received ordinary education will by and by find out ways and means of imparting our knowledge to others.

Swadeshi

At the ashram we hold that swadeshi is a universal law. A man's first duty is to his neighbor. This does not imply hatred for the foreigner or partiality for the fellow-countryman. Our capacity for service has obvious limits. We can serve even our neighbor with some difficulty. If every one of us duly performed his duty to his neighbor, no one in the world who needed assistance would be left unattended. Therefore one who serves his neighbor serves all the world. As a matter of fact there is in swadeshi no room for distinction between one's own and other people. To serve one's neighbor is to serve the world. Indeed it is the only way open to us of serving the world. One to whom the whole world is as his family should have the power of serving the universe without moving from his place. He can exercise this power only through service rendered to his neighbor. Tolstoy goes further and says that at present we are riding on other people's backs; it is enough only if we get down. This is another way of putting the same thing. No one can serve others without serving himself. And whoever tries to achieve his private ends without serving others harms himself as well as the world at large. The reason is obvious. All living beings are members one of another so that a person's every act has a beneficial or harmful influence on the whole world. We cannot see this, near-sighted as we are. The influence of a single act of an individual on the world may be negligible. But that influence is there all the same, and an awareness of this truth should make us realize our responsibility.

Swadeshi therefore does not involve any disservice to the foreigner. Still swadeshi does not reach everywhere, for that is impossible in the very nature of things. In trying to serve the world, one does not serve the world and fails to serve even the neighbor. In serving the neighbor one in effect serves the world. Only he who has performed his duty to his neighbor has the right to say, "All are akin to me." But if a person says, "All are akin to me," and neglecting his neighbor gives himself up to self-indulgence, he lives to himself alone.

We find some good men who leave their own place and move all over the world serving non-neighbors. They do nothing wrong, and their activity is not an exception to the law of swadeshi. Only their capacity for service is greater. To one man, only he who lives next door to him is his neighbor. For a second man his neighborhood is coextensive with his village and for a third with ten surrounding villages. Thus everyone serves according to his capacity. A common man cannot do uncommon work. Definitions are framed with an eye to him alone, and imply everything which is not contrary to their spirit. When he observes the law of swadeshi, the ordinary man does not think that he is doing service to any others. He deals with the neighboring producer, as it is convenient for him. But an occasion may arise when this is inconvenient. One who knows that swadeshi is the law of life will observe it even on such occasions. Many of us at present are not satisfied with the quality of goods made in India, and are tempted to buy foreign goods. It is therefore necessary to point out that swadeshi does not simply minister to our convenience but is a rule of life. Swadeshi has nothing to do with hatred of the foreigner. It can never be one's duty to wish or to do ill to others.

Khadi [local, handmade cloth] has been conceived as the symbol of swadeshi, because India has committed a heinous sin by giving it up and thus failing in the discharge of her natural duty.

The importance of khadi and the spinning-wheel first dawned on me in 1908, when I had no idea of what the wheel was like and did not even know the difference between the wheel and the loom. I had only a vague idea of the condition of India's villages, but still I clearly saw that the chief cause of their pauperization was the destruction of the spinning-wheel, and resolved that I would try to revive it when I returned to India.

I returned in 1915 with my mind full of these ideas. Swadeshi was one of the observances ever since the ashram was started. But none of us knew how to spin. We therefore rested content with setting up a handloom. Some of us still retained a liking for fine cloth. No swadeshi yarn of the requisite fineness for women's saris was available in the market. For a very short time therefore they were woven with foreign yarn. But we were soon able to obtain fine yarn from Indian mills.

It was no easy job even to set up the handloom at the ashram. None of us had the least idea of weaving. We obtained a loom and a weaver through friends. Maganlal Gandhi undertook to learn weaving.

I conducted experiments at the ashram and at the same time carried on swadeshi propaganda in the country. But it was like Hamlet without the Prince of Denmark so long as we could not spin yarn. At last however I discovered the spinning-wheel, found out spinners and introduced the wheel in the ashram. The whole story has been unfolded in the *Autobiography.*

But that did not mean that our difficulties were at an end. On the other hand they increased, since such of them as were hidden till now became manifest.

Touring in the country I saw that people would not take to the spinning-wheel as soon as they were told about it. I knew that not much money could be made by spinning, but I had no idea of how little it was. Then again the yarn that was spun would not at once be uniform as well as fine. Many could spin only coarse and weak yarn. Not all kinds of cotton were suitable for spinning. The cotton must be carded and made into slivers, and in carding much depended upon the condition of the cotton. Any and every spinning-wheel would not do. To revive the spinning wheel thus meant the launching of a big scheme. Money alone could not do the trick. As for manpower too, hundreds of workers would be needed, and these men should be ready to learn a new art, to be satisfied with a small salary and to live out their lives in villages. But even that was not enough. The rural atmosphere was surcharged with idleness and lack of faith and hope. The wheel could make no headway if this did not improve. Thus a successful revival of the wheel could be brought about only with an army of single-minded men and women equipped with infinite patience and strong faith.

At first I was alone in having this faith. Faith indeed was the only capital that I had, but I saw that if there is faith, everything else is added unto it. Faith enlightens the intellect and induces habits of industry. It was clear that all experiments should be conducted at and through the ashram which indeed existed for that very purpose. I realized that spinning should be the principal physical activity of the ashram. Thus only could it be reduced to a science. Therefore spinning was at last recognized as a *mahayajna* (primary sacrifice), and everyone who joined the ashram had to learn spinning and to spin regularly every day.

But *yajna* implies skill in action (*Bhagavad Gita*, II. 50). To spin some yarn somehow cannot be called a *yajna*. At first the rule was that the members should spin for at least half an hour every day. But it was soon found that if the spinning-wheel went out of order, one could not spin even a couple of yards in half an hour. Therefore the rule was modified and members were asked to spin at least 160 rounds, one round being equal to four feet. Again yarn was no good if it was not uniform as well as strong. Tests of strength and uniformity were therefore devised, and we have now made such progress that spinning yarn coarser than twenties [16,800 yards per pound of cotton] does not count as *yajna*.

But granted that good yarn is spun, who would make use of it? I was sure from the first that the person who did spinning as a sacrament must not use his own yarn, but I was unable to carry conviction to others. Where was the harm if the spinner paid the wages and purchased his yarn for himself? I deceived myself and agreed that one who paid the wages and bought his own yarn should be considered a spinning-sacrificer. This error has not still been rectified. Errors not dealt with with a strong hand at their first appearance tend to become permanent, and are difficult to eradicate like chronic diseases.

As a consequence of this *yajna*, spinning has made great

strides in India, but it has still to take root in each of our villages. The reason is obvious. My faith was not coupled with knowledge. Some knowledge was acquired after mistakes had been committed. Co-workers have joined me, but are too few for the great task in hand. There are hundreds of workers, but perhaps they have not in them the requisite faith and knowledge. The root being thus weak, one may not expect to enjoy the ripest fruit.

But for this I cannot find fault with anybody. The work is new and wide as the ocean and it bristles with difficulties. Therefore though the result of our activity is not gratifying, it is still sufficient for sustaining our faith. We have every right to hope for complete success. Faithful workers, men as well as women, have joined in adequate numbers and have accumulated a fund of valuable experience, so that this movement is certainly destined not to perish.

Khadi has given rise to quite a number of other activities at the ashram as well as elsewhere in the country which cannot here be dealt with at any length. Suffice it to say that cotton crops are raised, spinning-wheels are made, cloth is dyed, and simple hand-operated machines are manufactured for all the processes from ginning to weaving. These machines are being improved from time to time. The progress made in producing a more efficient type of spinning-wheel is a piece of poetry to my mind.

Removal of Untouchability

The ashram was founded in order to serve and if necessary to die in the service of truth. If therefore while holding that untouchability is a sinful thing, it did not do something positive in order to end it, it could hardly deserve the name of Satya-graha (adherence to truth) Ashram. Even in South Africa we recognized untouchability as a sin. When the ashram therefore was founded in India, removal of untouchability easily became one of its major activities.

Within a month of the foundation of the ashram, Dudabhai applied for admission along with his family. I had no idea that the testing time of the ashram would arrive so soon. Dudabhai's application was supported by Shri Amritlal Thakkar. I felt bound to admit a family which was recommended by him.

The arrival of Dudabhai was the signal for a storm breaking upon the placid atmosphere of the ashram. Kasturba, Maganlal Gandhi and Mrs. Maganlal [Gandhi's wife, son and daughter-in-law] had each of them some scruples in living with so-called untouchables. Things came to such a pass that Kasturba should either observe ashram rules or else leave the ashram. But the argument that a woman in following in her husband's footsteps incurs no sin appealed to her and she quieted down. I do not hold that a wife is bound to follow her husband in what she considers sinful. But I welcomed my wife's attitude in the present case, because I looked upon the removal of untouchability as a meritorious thing. No one could uphold untouchability and still live in the ashram. It would have been extremely painful to me if my wife had had to leave the ashram, seeing that she had been my companion all these days at the cost of great suffering. It was hard to be separated from her, but one must put up with every hardship that comes his way in the discharge of his duty. I had therefore no hesitation in accepting my wife's renunciation of untouchability not as an independent person but only as a faithful wife.

Maganlal Gandhi's case was harder than mine. He packed up his things and came to me to bid good-bye. But who was I to bid him good-bye? I put him on his guard. I told him that the ashram was his creation as much as mine, and would be destroyed if he left it. But he certainly did not want that it should perish. He did not need to seek my permission to leave an institution which he himself had brought into existence. But to leave the ashram should be something unthinkable for him. This appeal did not fall on deaf ears. Perhaps Maganlal had thought of leaving in order to give me a free hand. I could endure to be separated from all the world besides but not from Maganlal. I therefore suggested that he should go to Madras with family. He and his wife would learn more of weaving there and would have more time to ponder over the situation that had developed. So they went and lived in Madras for six months. They mastered the art of weaving and after mature consideration also washed their hearts clean of untouchability.

The internal storm thus blew over. But there was a storm outside the ashram too. The chief person who financed the ashram discontinued his assistance. There was even a possibility that the ashramites would not be allowed any more to draw water from the neighbor's well. But all difficulties were surmounted by and by. As regards finance, something happened which was not unlike Narasinha Mehta's *hundi* (bill of exchange) being honored at Dvaravati. A sum of thirteen thousand rupees was received from an unexpected source. Thus the ashram ordeal in keeping Dudabhai at any cost was not so severe as it might well have been. The ashram passed the test as regards its opposition to untouchability. "Untouchable" families come to the ashram freely and live in it. Dudabhai's daughter Lakshmi has become a full member of the family.

Three callings followed by the so-called untouchables are practiced in the ashram, and improved methods are devised in each. Everyone in the ashram has in turn to do sanitary service, which is looked upon not as a special calling but a universal duty. No outside labor is engaged for this work, which is carried on on lines suggested by Dr. Poore. Night-soil is buried in shallow trenches and is thus converted into manure in only a few days. Dr. Poore says that the soil is living up to a depth of twelve inches. Millions of bacteria are there to clean up dirt. Sunlight and air penetrate the ground to that depth. Therefore night-soil buried in the upper layer readily combines with the earth.

Closets are so constructed that they are free from smell and there is no difficulty in cleaning them. Everyone who visits them covers the night-soil with plenty of dry earth, so that the top is always dry.

Then again we have handloom weaving. Coarse khadi was manufactured in Gujarat by Harijan weavers only. The industry was almost on the verge of destruction, and many weavers were compelled to take up scavenging for a living. But now there has been a revival of this handicraft.

Thirdly we have tanning. We shall deal with it in the chapter on the ashram dairy.

The ashram does not believe in subcastes. There are no restrictions on interdining and all ashramites sit to dinner in the same line. But no propaganda in favor of interdining is carried on outside the ashram, as it is unnecessary for the removal of untouchability, which implies the lifting of bans imposed on Harijans in public institutions and discarding the superstition that a man is polluted by the touch of certain persons by reason of their birth in a particular caste. This disability can be removed by legislation. Interdining and intermarriage, however, are reforms of a different type which cannot be promoted by legislation or social pressure. The ashramites therefore feel themselves free to take permitted food with everyone else but do not carry on any such propaganda.

Schools are established and wells sunk for Harijans through the ashram which chiefly finds the finance for such activities. The real anti-untouchability work carried on in the ashram is the reformed conduct of the ashramites. There is no room in the ashram for any ideas of high and low.

However the ashram believes that varnas and ashramas are essential elements of Hinduism. Only it puts a different interpretation on these time-honored terms. Four varnas and four ashramas are an arrangement not peculiar to Hinduism but capable of world-wide application, and a universal rule, the breach of which has involved humanity in numerous disasters. The four ashramas are *brahmacharya, garhasthya, vanaprasthya* and sannyasa. *Brahmacharya* is the stage during which men as well as women prosecute their studies, and should not only observe *brahmacharya* but should also be free from any other burden except that of studies. This lasts till at least the twenty-fifth year, when the student becomes a householder if he wishes. Almost all the students thus become householders. But this stage should close at the age of fifty. During that period the householder enjoys the pleasures of life, makes money, practices a profession and rears a family. From fifty to seventy-five wife and husband should live apart and wholly devote themselves to the service of the people. They must leave their families and try to look upon the world as a big family. During the last twenty-five years they should become sannyasis, live apart, set to the people an example of ideal religious life and maintain themselves with whatever the people choose to give them. It is clear that society as a whole would be elevated if many carried out this scheme in their lives.

So far as I am aware, the ashrama arrangement is unknown outside India, but even in India it has practically disappeared at present. There is no such thing now as *brahmacharya*, which is intended to be the foundation of life. For the rest we have sannyasis, most of them such only in name, with nothing of sannyasa about them except the orange robe. Many of them are ignorant, and some who have acquired learning are not knowers of Brahman but fanatics. There are some honorable exceptions but even these well-conducted monks lack the luster we love to associate with sannyasa. It is possible that some real sannyasis lead a solitary life. But it is obvious that sannyasa as a stage in life has fallen into desuetude. A society which is served by able sannyasis would not be poor in spirit, unprovided even with the necessaries of life, and politically dependent, as Hindu society is at present. If sannyasa were with us a living thing, it would exert a powerful influence on neighboring faiths, for the sannyasi is a servant not only of Hinduism but of all the faiths of mankind But we can never hope to see such sannyasis unless *brahmacharya* is observed in the country. As for *vanaprasthya*, there is no trace of it. The last stage we have to consider is that of the householder. But our householders are given to unregulated self-indulgence. Householders in the absence of the three other ashramas live like brutes. Self-restraint is the one thing which differentiates man from beast, but it is practiced no longer.

The ashram is engaged in the great endeavor to resuscitate the four ashramas. It is like an ant trying to lift a bag of sugar. This effort though apparently ridiculous is part of the ashram quest of truth. All the inmates of the ashram therefore observe *brahmacharya*. Permanent members must observe it for life. All the inmates are not members in this sense. Only a few are members, the rest are students. If this effort is crowned with success, we may hope to see a revival of the ashrama scheme of life. The sixteen years during which the ashram has functioned are not a sufficiently long period for the assessment of results. I have no idea of the time when such assessment will be possible. I can only say that there is nothing like dissatisfaction with the progress achieved up to date.

If the ashrama scheme has broken down, the plight of the varnas is equally bad. At first there were four varnas ([professional] classes); but now there are innumerable sections or only one. If we take it that there are as many varnas as there are castes and subcastes, their name is legion; on the other hand if, as I think, varnas have nothing to do with caste, there is only a single varna left and that is the Shudra. We are here not finding fault with anybody but only stating the facts of the case. Shudras are those who serve and are dependent upon others. India is a dependency; therefore every Indian is a Shudra. The cultivator does not own his land, the merchant his merchandise. There is hardly a Kshatriya or a Brahmin [the traditional warrior and priestly classes] who possesses the virtues which the Shastras attribute to his varna.

My impression is that there was no idea of high and low when the varna system was discovered. No one is high and no one is low in this world; therefore he who thinks he belongs to a high class is never high-class, and he who believes himself to be low is merely the victim of ignorance. He has been taught by his masters that he is low. If a Brahmin has knowledge, those who are without it will respect him as a matter of course. But if he is puffed up by the respect thus shown to him and imagines himself to belong to a high class, he directly ceases to be a Brahmin. Virtue will always command respect, but when the man of virtue thinks much of himself, his virtue ceases to have any significance for the world. Talents of all kinds are a trust and must be utilized for the benefit of society. The individual has no right to live unto himself. Indeed it is impossible to live unto oneself. We fully live unto ourselves when we live unto society.

No matter what was the position in ancient times, no one can nowadays go through life claiming to belong to a high class. Society will not willingly admit any such claim to superiority, but only under duress. The world is now wide awake. This awakening has perhaps given rise to some license, but even so public opinion is not now prepared to accept any distinctions of high and low, which are being attacked on all sides. There is ever increasing realization that all are equal as human souls. The fact that we are all the creatures of one God rules out all ideas of high and low. When we say that no one is high-born or low-born, it does not mean that all have or ought to have equal talents. All have not equal talents, equal property or equal opportunities. Still all are equal like brothers and sisters of different dispositions, abilities and ages.

If therefore the varna system is a spiritual arrangement, there cannot be any place in it for high and low.

Thus there are four varnas, all equal in status, and they are determined by birth. They can be changed by a person choosing another profession, but if varnas are not as a rule determined by birth, they tend to lose all meaning.

The varna system is ethical as well as economic. It recognizes the influence of previous lives and of heredity. All are not born with equal powers and similar tendencies. Neither the parents nor the State can measure the intelligence of each child. But there would be no difficulty if each child is prepared for the profession indicated by heredity, environment and the influence of former lives; no time would be lost in fruitless experimentation, there would be no soul-killing competition, a spirit of contentment would pervade society and there would be no struggle for existence.

The varna system implies the obliteration of all distinctions of high and low. If the carpenter is held to be superior to the shoemaker and the pleader or doctor is superior to both of them, no one would willingly become a shoemaker or carpenter and all would try to become pleaders or doctors. They would be entitled to do so and to be praised for doing so. That is to say, the varna system would be looked upon as an evil and abolished as such.

But when it is suggested that everyone should practice his father's profession, the suggestion is coupled with the condition that the practitioner of every profession will earn only a living wage and no more. If the carpenter earns more than a shoemaker and the pleader or doctor more than both, everyone would become a lawyer or doctor. Such is the case at present, with the result that hatred has increased and there are more lawyers and doctors than are necessary. It may be that society needs the lawyer or doctor even as it needs the shoemaker and the carpenter. These four professions are here taken only as illustrations and for comparison. It would be irrelevant to stop to consider whether society has particular need or no need at all for this, that or the other profession.

This principle then is an integral part of the varna system, that learning is not a trade and may not be used in order to amass riches. Therefore in so far as his ministrations may be necessary, the lawyer or doctor ought by practicing his profession to earn only a living wage. And such was actually the case formerly. The village vaidya (physician) did not earn more than the carpenter but only a living wage. In short the emoluments of all crafts and professions should be equal and amount to a living wage. The number of varnas has no sanctity about it; their value is due to the fact that they define the duties of man. Varnas may be supposed to be one or more just as we like. The scriptures enumerate four of them. But when once we have assigned equal status to all, it makes little difference whether we think that there are four varnas or that there is only one.

Such is the varna system which the ashram is trying to resuscitate. It is like Dame Partington with her mop, trying to push back the Atlantic Ocean. I have already mentioned its two fundamental principles, namely, that there are no high and low, and everyone is entitled to a living wage, the living wage being the same for all. In so far as these principles win acceptance, they will render a positive service to society.

It may be objected that if such a plan is accepted there will be no incentive for the acquisition of knowledge. But the object with which knowledge is acquired nowadays tends to corrupt it, and therefore the absence of an incentive will be entirely beneficial. Knowledge truly so called is intended for one's salvation, that is to say, service of mankind. Whoever has a desire to render service will certainly try to equip himself with the requisite knowledge, and his knowledge will be an ornament to himself as well as to society. Again when the temptation to amass riches is removed, there will be a change for the better in the curriculum of studies as well as in the methods of education. There is much misuse of knowledge at present. This misuse will be reduced to the minimum in the "new order."

Even then there will be scope for competition in trying to be good and helpful. And there will be no discontent or disorder as all will receive a living wage.

Varna is wrongly understood today. That wrong understanding must make way for the principles outlined above. Untouchability must go, and varnas should have nothing to do with interdining or intermarriage. A person will dine with and marry whom he likes. But as a rule he will marry someone who belongs to the same varna as himself. But if he marries a person belonging to another varna, his act will not count as a sin. A person will be boycotted not by the varna but by society at large when his conduct justifies such a measure. Society will be better constituted than it is at present, and the impurity and hypocrisy which infest it now will be dislodged.

Agriculture

This department of ashram activities owes its existence to Maganlal Gandhi. But for him I would not have had the courage to take up agriculture at all, although an ashram without it would be something like Hamlet without the Prince of Denmark. For we had not the requisite skill and environment for it as I thought. Agriculture is a very big undertaking and would call for a lot of land, money and man-power. I was afraid that it would distract our attention from other necessary things which could be done and would not wait. But Maganlal was insistent and I yielded to him. "Let me do it," he said, "if only for my own diversion." Maganlal hardly ever argued with me.

He thought it his duty to carry out my ideas. If he did not understand them or if he disagreed, he would tell me so. If even then I stuck to my plans, he would take it that they were correct, and execute them. In fact he believed that an ashram without agriculture was something not to be thought of, and he would have had to make out a case for his belief. Instead he put forward the supreme argument of love and the ashram launched upon agriculture. Most of the trees in the ashram were planted by Maganlal or at his instance.

I still have my doubts about agriculture. Even today I cannot claim that it is a full-fledged ashram activity. But I am not sorry for what little cultivation of the soil is done in the ashram. A considerable amount of money has been sunk in it. It is not possible to show that it is self-supporting. However I am inclined to think that this much farming was necessary for the ashram. No farming, no ashram; for it must grow its own vegetables and fruit as far as possible. Indeed later on Maganlal took a vow that he would restrict himself to the use of ashram-grown vegetables. An ashram should acquire the capacity to grow its own food grains and grass for the cattle. It may not carry on agricultural research, but an ashram without its farm would look like a face without the nose.

The ashram farm is only in an experimental stage. It has not much to teach anybody. It is intended to impart only an elementary knowledge of agriculture. At first there was not a single tree in the ashram, but now there are many trees, planted with a view to their utility. Vegetables are grown as well as some fruit and fodder. Night-soil is used as manure with satisfactory results.

Ancient ploughs are used as well as modern improved models, water is pumped from wells by methods which can be

followed in villages. We are rather partial to ancient imple-
ments which are suitable for the poor farmer. They may be
susceptible of some slight improvement, but nothing definite
can be said about it, as the ashram has not the time to apply
its mind to the subject.

Dairy

The ashram ideal is to do without milk, as it holds that the
milk of animals, like meat, is no food for mankind. For a year
and more no milk or ghee was used in the ashram, but as the
health of the children as well as the adults suffered under this
regimen, first ghee and then milk had to be added to the ashram
dietary. And when this was done, it was clear that we must
keep cattle in the ashram.

The ashram believes in cow-protection as a religious duty.
But cow-protection savors of pride. Man is incompetent to
"protect" animals, being himself in need of the protection of
God who is the protector of all life. The term was therefore
replaced by cow-service. But as the experiment of doing without milk or ghee and thus serving the cow without any selfish
considerations did not succeed, cattle were kept in the ashram.
We had buffaloes as well as cows and bullocks at first, as we
had not yet realized that it was our duty to keep cows and
bullocks only to the exclusion of the buffalo.

But it became clear day by day that cow-service alone at
present stood for the service of all sub-human life. It is the
first step beyond which we have not the resources to go for the
time being. Again cow-slaughter is very often the cause of
Hindu-Muslim tension. The ashram believes that it is not the
duty of a Hindu, nor has he the right, to take away a Muslim's

cow by force. There is no service to or protection of the cow in trying to save her by force; on the other hand it only expedites slaughter. Hindus can save the cow and her progeny only by doing their duty to her and thus making her slaughter a costly act which no one can afford to do. Hindu society does not discharge this duty at present.

The cow suffers from neglect. The buffalo gives more and richer milk than the cow, and keeping a buffalo costs less than keeping a cow. Again if the buffalo brings forth a bull calf, people do not care what becomes of him because buffalo "protection" or "service" is not a religious duty for them. Hindu society has thus been short-sighted, cowardly, ignorant and selfish enough to neglect the cow and has installed the buffalo in her place, injuring both of them in the process. The buffalo's interest is not served by our keeping her, but lies in her freedom. To keep the buffalo means torturing its bull calf to death. This is not the case in all the provinces, but where the buffalo bull is useless for agricultural purposes, as in Gujarat, for instance, it is doomed to a premature death.

On account of these considerations, buffaloes were disposed of and the ashram now insists on keeping cows and bullocks only. Improvement of breed, increasing the quantity and enriching the quality of milk by giving various feeds, the art of preserving milk and extracting butter from it more easily, least painful methods of castrating bull calves, all these things are attended to. It is in an experimental stage, but the ashram does believe that the cow will pay for its keep if she is well treated and all her products are fully utilized.

Many perhaps are not aware that a man cannot simply afford to keep a cow, and slaughter is inevitable so long as that is the case. Mankind is not so benevolent that it will die to save the cow or allow it to live on itself as a parasite. The cattle population at present is so large that if it is well fed, the human population will not have enough food left for itself. We must therefore prove the proposition that the cow, if well kept, is capable of greater production.

If this proposition is to be proved, Hindu society must discard some superstitions masquerading as religion. Hindus do not utilize the bones, etc., of dead cows; they do not care what becomes of cattle when they are dead. Instead of looking upon the occupation of a tanner as sacred, they think it unclean. Emaciated cattle are exported to and slaughtered in Australia where their bones are converted into manure, their flesh into meat extract and their hides into boots and shoes. The meat extract, the manure and the shoes are then re-exported to India and used without any compunction.

This stupidity makes for the destruction of the cow, and puts the country to huge economic losses. This is not religion but the negation of it. Tanning has therefore been introduced in the ashram. None of us is still a skilled tanner. No tanner from outside who would keep the ashram rules has been available. But all the same tanning is an integral part of ashram industry and we have every hope that it will be developed and propagated like spinning. The cow will cease to be a burden to the country only if dead cattle are utilized. Even then there will not be any profits. Religion is never opposed to economics, but it is always ranged in opposition to profits. . . .

Education

This word is here used in a special as well as the current sense. The ashram experiment in education was a trial for us as nothing else was.

We saw at once that the women and children in the ashram should be taught to read and write, and a little later on that there should be similar facilities for even the illiterate men that came to the ashram. Those who had already joined the ashram could not undertake to teach. If capable teachers were to be attracted to the ashram, the rule of *brahmacharya* had to be relaxed in their case. The ashram was therefore divided into two sections, the teachers' quarters and the ashram proper.

Human beings cannot overcome their weakness all at once. As soon as the two sections came into being, a feeling of superiority and inferiority poisoned the ashram atmosphere in spite of all our efforts to scotch it. The ashramites developed spiritual pride, which the teachers could not tolerate. This pride was an obstacle in the attainment of the ashram ideal and therefore an aspect of untruth as well. If brahmacharya was to be observed in its perfection, the division was inevitable. But the brahmacharis had no reason to think too highly of themselves. It may be that the brahmacharis who sinned mentally in spite of themselves were retrogressing while those who did not claim to be brahmacharis but liked brahmacharya were making progress. This was clear to the intellect but it was not easy for all of us to put it into practice.

Then again there were differences of opinion as regards the method of education which gave rise to difficulties in administration. There were bitter discussions, but at last all calmed down and learned the lesson of forbearance. This was in my view a triumph of truth, the goal of all ashram endeavor. Those who held divergent views harbored no evil intentions in their minds, and were indeed grieved at the divergence. They wished to practice truth as they saw it. Their partiality for their own standpoint came in the way of their giving due weight to the arguments of their opponents. Hence the quarrels which put our charity to a severe test.

I have my own perhaps peculiar views on education which have not been accepted by my colleagues in full. They are:

1. Young boys and girls should have coeducation till they are eight years of age.
2. Their education should mainly consist in manual training under the supervision of an educationist.
3. The special aptitudes of each child should be recognized in determining the kind of work he or she should do.
4. The reasons for every process should be explained when the process is being carried on.
5. General knowledge should be imparted to each child as he begins to understand things. Learning to read or write should come later.
6. The child should first be taught to draw simple geometrical figures, and when he has learnt to draw these with ease, he should be taught to write the alphabet. If this is done he will write a good hand from the very first.
7. Reading should come before writing. The letters should be treated as pictures to be recognized and later on to be copied.
8. A child taught on these lines will have acquired considerable knowledge according to his capacity by the time he is eight.
9. Nothing should be taught to a child by force.

10. He should be interested in everything taught to him.

11. Education should appear to the child like play. Play is an essential part of education.

12. All education should be imparted through the mother tongue.

13. The child should be taught Hindi-Urdu as the national language, before he learns letters.

14. Religious education is indispensable and the child should get it by watching the teacher's conduct and by hearing him talk about it.

15. Nine to sixteen constitutes the second stage in the child's education.

16. It is desirable that boys and girls should have coeducation during the second stage also as far as possible.

17. Hindu children should now be taught Sanskrit, and Muslim children Arabic.

18. Manual training should be continued during the second stage. Literary education should be allotted more time according to necessity.

19. The boys during this stage should be taught their parents' vocation in such a way that they will by their own choice obtain their livelihood by practicing the hereditary craft. This does not apply to the girls.

20. During this stage the child should acquire a general knowledge of world history and geography, botany, astronomy, arithmetic, geometry, and algebra.

21. Each child should now be taught to sew and how

to cook.

22. Sixteen to twenty-five is the third stage, during which every young person should have an education according to his or her wishes and circumstances.

23. During the second stage (9-16) education should be self-supporting; that is, the child, all the time that he is learning is working upon some industry, the proceeds of which will meet the expenditure of the school.

24. Production starts from the very beginning, but during the first stage it does not still catch up with the expenditure.

25. Teachers should be paid not very high salaries but only a living wage. They should be inspired by a spirit of service. It is a despicable thing to take any Tom, Dick or Harry as a teacher in the primary stage. All teachers should be men of character.

26. Big and expensive buildings are not necessary for educational institutions.

27. English should be taught only as one of several languages. As Hindi is the national language, English is to be used in dealing with other nations and international commerce.

As for women's education I am not sure whether it should be different from men's and when it should begin. But I am strongly of opinion that women should have the same facilities as men and even special facilities where necessary.

There should be night schools for illiterate adults. But I

do not think that they must be taught the three R's; they must be helped to acquire general knowledge through lectures, etc., and if they wish, we should arrange to teach them the three R's also.

Experiments in the ashram have convinced us of one thing, viz., that industry in general and spinning in particular should have pride of place in education, which must be largely self-supporting as well as related to and tending to the betterment of rural life.

In these experiments we have achieved the largest measure of success with the women, who have imbibed the spirit of freedom and self-confidence as no other class of women have done to my knowledge. This success is due to the ashram atmosphere. Women in the ashram are not subject to any restraint which is not imposed on the men as well. They are placed on a footing of absolute equality with the men in all activities. Not a single ashram task is assigned to the women to the exclusion of the men. Cooking is attended to by both. Women are of course exempted from work which is beyond their strength; otherwise men and women work together everywhere. No matter from where she has come, a woman, as soon as she enters the ashram, breathes the air of freedom and casts out all fear from her mind. And I believe that the ashram observance of brahmacharya has made a big contribution to this state of things. Adult girls live in the ashram as virgins. We are aware that this experiment is fraught with risk but we feel that no awakening among women is possible without incurring it.

Women cannot make any progress so long as there are child marriages. All girls are supposed to be in duty bound to marry and that too before menstruation commences, and widow remarriage is not permitted. Women, therefore, when they join the ashram, are told that these social customs are wrong and irreligious. But they are not shocked as they find the ashram practicing what it preaches.

Not much of what is usually called education will be observed in the ashram. Still we find that the old as well as the young, women as well as men, are eager to acquire knowledge and complain that they have no time for it. This is a good sign. Many who join the ashram are not educated or even interested in education. Some of them can hardly read or write. They had no desire for progress so long as they had not joined the ashram. But when they have lived in the ashram for a little while, they conceive a desire for increasing their knowledge. This is a great thing, as to create a desire for knowledge is very often the first step to be taken. But I do not regret it very much that there are insufficient facilities in the ashram calculated to satisfy this desire. The observances kept in the ashram will perhaps prevent a sufficient number of qualified teachers from joining it. We must therefore rest satisfied with such ashramites as can be trained to teach. The numerous activities of the ashram may come in the way of their acquiring the requisite qualifications at all, or at an early date. But it does not matter much, as the desire for knowledge can be satisfied later as well as sooner, being independent of a time-limit. Real education begins after a child has left school. One who has appreciated the value of studies is a student all his life. His knowledge must increase from day to day while he is discharging his duty in a conscientious manner. And this is well understood in the ashram.

The superstition that no education is possible without a teacher is an obstacle in the path of educational progress. A man's real teacher is himself. And nowadays there are numerous aids available for self-education. A diligent person can easily acquire knowledge about many things by himself and obtain the assistance of a teacher when it is needed. Experience is the biggest of all schools. Quite a number of crafts cannot be learnt at school but only in the workshop. Knowledge of these acquired at school is often only parrot-like. Other subjects can be learnt with the help of books. Therefore what adults need is not so much a school as a thirst for knowledge, diligence and self-confidence.

The education of children is primarily a duty to be discharged by the parents. Therefore the creation of a vital educational atmosphere is more important than the foundation of numerous schools. When once this atmosphere has been established on a firm footing the schools will come in due course.

This is the ashram ideal of education which has been realized to some extent, as every department of ashram activity is a veritable school.

Satyagraha

The various activities of the ashram have already been covered more or less. The ashram came into existence to seek the truth by adhering to truthful conduct. And while doing so, if we are required to use the weapon of satyagraha, the ashram may experiment with it, may explore its rules and limitations. The broad framework of these rules has also been discussed.

But what are the limits of satyagraha? When can this weapon be employed with vigor? Man's adherence to truth is also satyagraha. It is not this form of satyagraha that is being discussed here. I am examining its utility as a weapon against an opponent.

Such satyagraha can be offered against associates, relatives, society, the State and the world. At the root of it   [This section ends here abruptly.]

From Yeravda Mandir: Essays on the Observances

During my incarceration in 1930 in the Yeravda Central Prison, I wrote weekly letters to the Satyagraha Ashram, containing a cursory examination of the principal ashram observances. As the ashram influence had already traveled beyond its geographical limits, copies of the letters were multiplied for distribution. They were written in Gujarati. There was a demand for translation into Hindi and other Indian languages, and also into English. Shri Valji Desai gave a fairly full translation in English. But seeing me in possession of comparative leisure during the recurrent incarceration, he has sent me his translation for revision. I have gone through it carefully, and touched up several passages to bring out my meaning more to my liking. I need hardly add that if I was writing anew for the English reader, perhaps I should write a wholly new thing. But that would be going beyond my commission. And perhaps it is as well that even the English reader has the trend of my thought as expressed to the inmates of the ashram, and in the year 1930. I have therefore taken the least liberty with the original argument.

Yeravda Central Prison
March 6, 1932

Truth

I deal with truth first of all, as the Satyagraha Ashram owes its very existence to the pursuit and the attempted practice of truth.

The word *satya*, truth, is derived from *sat*, which means "being." Nothing is or exists in reality except truth. That is why *sat* or truth is perhaps the most important name of God. In fact it is more correct to say that truth is God, than to say that God is truth. But as we cannot do without a ruler or a general, such names of God as "King of Kings" or "The Almighty" are and will remain generally current. On deeper thinking, however, it will be realized, that *sat or satya* is the only correct and fully significant name for God.

And where there is truth, there also is knowledge which is true. Where there is no truth, there can be no true knowledge. That is why the word *chit* or knowledge is associated with the name of God. And where there is true knowledge, there is always bliss, *ananda*. There sorrow has no place. And even as truth is eternal, so is the bliss derived from it. Hence we know God as *Sat-chit-ananda*, one who combines in himself truth, knowledge and bliss.

Devotion to this truth is the sole justification for our existence. All our activities should be centered in truth. Truth should be the very breath of our life. When once this stage in the pilgrim's progress is reached, all other rules of correct living will come without effort, and obedience to them will be instinctive. But without truth it is impossible to observe any principles or rules in life.

Generally speaking, observation of the law of truth is understood merely to mean that we must speak the truth. But we in the ashram should understand the word *satya* or truth in a much wider sense. There should be truth in thought, truth in speech, and truth in action. To the man who has realized this truth in its fullness, nothing else remains to be known, because all knowledge is necessarily included in it. What is not included in it is not truth, and so not true knowledge; and there can be no inward peace without true knowledge. If we once learn how to apply this never-failing test of truth, we will at once be able to find out what is worth doing, what is worth seeing, what is worth reading.

But how is one to realize this truth, which may be likened to the philosopher's stone or the cow of plenty? By single-minded devotion, *abhyasa*, and indifference to all other interests in life, *vairagya*, replies the *Bhagavadgita*. In spite, however, of such devotion, what may appear as truth to one person will often appear as untruth to another person. But that need not worry the seeker. Where there is honest effort, it will be realized that what appear to be different truths are like the countless and apparently different leaves of the same tree. Does not God himself appear to different individuals in different aspects? Yet we know that he is one. But truth is the right designation of God. Hence there is nothing wrong in every man following truth according to his lights. Indeed it is his duty to do so. Then if there is a mistake on the part of any one so following truth, it will be automatically set right. For the quest of truth involves *tapas*—self-suffering, sometimes even unto death. There can be no place in it for even a trace of self-interest. In such selfless search for truth nobody can lose his bearings for long. Directly he takes to the wrong path he stumbles, and is thus redirected to the right path. Therefore the pursuit of truth is true *bhakti*, devotion. It is the path that leads to God. There is no place in it for cowardice, no place for defeat. It is the talisman by which death itself becomes the portal to life eternal.

In this connection it would be well to ponder over the lives and examples of Harishchandra, Prahlad, Ramachandra, Imam Hasan and Imam Husain, the Christian saints, etc. How beautiful it would be if all of us, young and old, men and women, devoted ourselves wholly to truth in all that we might do in our waking hours, whether working, eating, drinking or playing, till dissolution of the body makes us one with truth? God as truth has been, for me, a treasure beyond price; may he be so to every one of us.

Ahimsa or Love

We saw last week how the path of truth is as narrow as it is straight. Even so is that of ahimsa. It is like balancing oneself on the edge of a sword. By concentration an acrobat can walk on a rope. But the concentration required to tread the path of truth and ahimsa is far greater. The slightest inattention brings one tumbling to the ground. One can realize truth and ahimsa only by ceaseless striving.

But it is impossible for us to realize perfect truth so long as we are imprisoned in this mortal frame. We can only visualize it in our imagination. We cannot, through the instrumentality of this ephemeral body, see face to face truth which is eternal. That is why in the last resort we must depend on faith.

It appears that the impossibility of full realization of truth in this mortal body led some ancient seeker after truth to the appreciation of ahimsa. The question which confronted him was, "Shall I bear with those who create difficulties for me, or shall I destroy them?" The seeker realized that he who went on destroying others did not make headway but simply stayed where he was, while the man who suffered those who created difficulties marched ahead, and at times even took the others with him. The first act of destruction taught him that the truth which was the object of his quest was not outside himself but within. Hence the more he took to violence, the more he receded from truth. For in fighting the imagined enemy without, he neglected the enemy within.

We punish thieves, because we think they harass us. They may leave us alone; but they will only transfer their attentions to another victim. This other victim however is also a human being, ourselves in a different form, and so we are caught in a vicious circle. The trouble from thieves continues to increase, as they think it is their business to steal. In the end we see that it is better to endure the thieves than to punish them. The forbearance may even bring them to their senses. By enduring them we realize that thieves are not different from ourselves; they are our brethren, our friends, and may not be punished. But whilst we may bear with the thieves, we may not endure the infliction. That would only induce cowardice. So we realize a further duty.

Since we regard the thieves as our kith and kin, they must be made to realize the kinship. And so we must take pains to devise ways and means of winning them over. This is the path of ahimsa. It may entail continuous suffering and the cultivating of endless patience. Given these two conditions, the thief is bound in the end to turn away from his evil ways. Thus step by step we learn how to make friends with all the world; we realize the greatness of God—of truth. Our peace of mind increases in spite of suffering, we become braver and more enterprising; we understand more clearly the difference between what is everlasting and what is not; we learn how to distinguish between what is our duty and what is not. Our pride melts away, and we become humble. Our worldly attachments diminish, and the evil within us diminishes from day to day.

Ahimsa is not the crude thing it has been made to appear. Not to hurt any living thing is no doubt a part of ahimsa. But it is its least expression. The principle of ahimsa is hurt by every evil thought, by undue haste, by lying, by hatred, by wishing ill to anybody. It is also violated by our holding on to what the world needs. But the world needs even what we eat day by day. In the place where we stand there are millions of microorganisms to whom the place belongs, and who are hurt by our presence there. What should we do then? Should we commit suicide? Even that is no solution, if we believe, as we do, that so long as the spirit is attached to the flesh, on every destruction of the body it weaves for itself another. The body will cease to be only when we give up all attachment to it. This freedom from all attachment is the realization of God as truth.

Such realization cannot be attained in a hurry. The body does not belong to us. While it lasts, we must use it as a trust handed over to our charge. Treating in this way the things of the flesh, we may one day expect to become free from the burden of the body. Realizing the limitations of the flesh, we must strive day by day towards the ideal, with what strength we have in us.

It is perhaps clear from the foregoing, that without ahimsa it is not possible to seek and find truth. Ahimsa and truth are so intertwined that it is practically impossible to disentangle and separate them. They are like the two sides of a coin, or rather, of a smooth, unstamped metallic disc. Who can say, which is the obverse, and which is the reverse? Nevertheless ahimsa is the means; truth is the end. Means to be means must always be within our reach, and so ahimsa is our supreme duty. If we take care of the means, we are bound to reach the end sooner or later. When once we have grasped this point, final victory is beyond question. Whatever difficulties we encounter, whatever apparent reverses we sustain, we may not give up the quest for truth which alone is, being God Himself.

Brahmacharya or Chastity

The third among our observances is *brahmacharya.* As a matter of fact all observances are deducible from truth, and are meant to subserve it. The man who is wedded to truth and worships truth alone, proves unfaithful to her if he applies his talents to anything else. How then can he minister to the senses? A man, whose activities are wholly consecrated to the realization of truth, which requires utter selflessness, can have no time for the selfish purpose of begetting children and running a household. Realization of truth through self-gratification should, after what has been said before, appear a contradiction in terms.

If we look at it from the standpoint of ahimsa (non-violence), we find that the fulfillment of ahimsa is impossible without utter selflessness. Ahimsa means universal love. If a man gives his love to one woman, or a woman to one man, what is there left for all the world besides? It simply means, "We two first, and the devil take all the rest of them." As a faithful wife must be prepared to sacrifice her all for the sake of her husband, and a faithful husband for the sake of his wife, it is clear that such persons cannot rise to the height of universal love, or look upon all mankind as kith and kin. For they have created a boundary wall round their love. The larger their family, the farther are they from universal love. Hence one who would obey the law of ahimsa cannot marry, not to speak of gratification outside the marital bond.

Then what about people who are already married? Will they never be able to realize truth? Can they never offer up their all at the altar of humanity? There is a way out for them. They can behave as if they were not married. Those who have enjoyed this happy condition will be able to bear me out. Many have to my knowledge successfully tried the experiment. If the married couple can think of each other as brother and sister, they are freed for universal service. The very thought that all the women in the world are his sisters, mothers or daughters will at once ennoble a man and snap his chains. The husband and wife do not lose anything here, but only add to their resources and even to their family. Their love becomes free from the impurity of lust and so grows stronger. With the disappearance of this impurity, they can serve each other better, and the occasions for quarreling become fewer. There are more occasions for quarreling where the love is selfish and bounded.

If the foregoing argument is appreciated, a consideration of the physical benefits of chastity becomes a matter of secondary importance. How foolish it is intentionally to dissipate vital energy in sensual enjoyment! It is a grave misuse to fritter away for physical gratification that which is given to man and woman for the full development of their bodily and mental powers. Such misuse is the root cause of many a disease.

Brahmacharya, like all other observances, must be observed in thought, word and deed. We are told in the *Gita*, and experience will corroborate the statement, that the foolish man, who appears to control his body but is nursing evil thoughts in his mind, makes a vain effort. It may be harmful to suppress the body if the mind is at the same time allowed to go astray. Where the mind wanders, the body must follow sooner or later. It is necessary here to appreciate a distinction. It is one thing to allow the mind to harbor impure thoughts; it is a different thing altogether if it strays among them in spite of ourselves. Victory will be ours in the end if we non-cooperate with the mind in its evil wanderings.

We experience, every moment of our lives, that often while the body is subject to our control, the mind is not. This physical control should never be relaxed, and in addition we must put forth a constant endeavor to bring the mind under control. We can do nothing more, nothing less. If we give way to the mind, the body and the mind will pull different ways, and we shall be false to ourselves. Body and mind may be said to go together, so long as we continue to resist the approach of every evil thought.

The observance of *brahmacharya* has been believed to be very difficult, almost impossible. In trying to find a reason for this belief, we see that the term *brahmacharya* has been taken in a narrow sense. Mere control of animal passion has been thought to be tantamount to observing *brahmacharya*. I feel that this conception is incomplete and wrong. *Brahmacharya* means control of all the organs of sense. He who attempts to control only one organ, and allows all the others free play, is bound to find his effort futile. To hear suggestive stories with the ears, to see suggestive sights with the eyes, to taste stimulating food with the tongue, to touch exciting things with the hands, and then at the same time to expect to control the only remaining organ is like putting one's hands in the fire and expecting to escape being burnt. He therefore who is resolved to control the one must be likewise determined to control the rest.

I have always felt that much harm has been done by the narrow definition of *brahmacharya*. If we practice simultaneous self-control in all directions, the attempt will be scientific and possible of success. Perhaps the palate is the chief sinner. That is why in the ashram we have assigned to control of the palate a separate place among our observances.

Let us remember the root meaning of *brahmacharya*. *Charya* means course of conduct; *brahma-charya* conduct adapted to the search of *Brahma*, i. e. truth. From this etymological meaning arises the special meaning, control of all the senses. We must entirely forget the incomplete definition which restricts itself to the sexual aspect only.

Control of the Palate

Control of the palate is very closely connected with the observance of *brahmacharya*. I have found from experience that the observance of celibacy becomes comparatively easy if one acquires mastery over the palate. This does not figure among the observances of time-honored recognition. Could it be because even great sages found it difficult to achieve? In the Satyagraha Ashram we have elevated it to the rank of an independent observance, and must therefore consider it by itself.

Food has to be taken as we take medicine, that is, without thinking whether it is palatable or otherwise, and only in quantities limited to the needs of the body. Just as medicine taken in too small a dose does not take effect or the full effect, and as too large a dose injures the system, so it is with food. It is therefore a breach of this observance to take anything just for its pleasant taste. It is equally a breach to take too much of what one finds to one's taste. From this it follows, that to put salt in one's food in order to increase or modify its flavor or in order to cure its insipidity, is a breach of the observance. But the addition is not a breach if it is considered necessary for health to have a certain proportion of salt with food. Of course it would be sheer hypocrisy to add salt or any other thing to our food, deluding ourselves that it is necessary for the system if, as a matter of fact, it is not.

Developing along these lines we find we have to give up many things that we have been enjoying, as they are not needed for nutrition. And one who thus gives up a multitude of eatables will acquire self-control in the natural course of things. This subject has received such scant attention that choice of food with this observance in view is a very difficult matter.

Parents, out of false affection, give their children a variety of foods, ruin their constitutions, and create in them artificial tastes. When they grow up, they have diseased bodies and perverted tastes. The evil consequences of this early indulgence dog us at every step; we waste much money and fall an easy prey to the medicine man.

Most of us, instead of keeping the organs of sense under control, become their slaves. An experienced physician once observed that he had never seen a healthy man. The body is injured every time that one over-eats, and the injury can be partially repaired only by fasting.

No one need take fright at my observations, or give up the effort in despair. The taking of a vow does not mean that we are able to observe it completely from the very beginning; it does mean constant and honest effort in thought, word and deed with a view to its fulfillment. We must not practice self-deception by resorting to some make-believe. To degrade or cheapen an ideal for our convenience is to practice untruth and to lower ourselves. To understand an ideal and then to make a Herculean effort to reach it, no matter how difficult it is—this is *purushartha*, manly endeavor. One who at all times fulfills the key observances in their perfection has nothing else left for him to do in this world; he is *bhagavan*, perfect man, he is a *yogi*. We humble seekers can but put forth a slow but steady effort, which is sure to win divine grace for us in God's good time, and all artificial tastes will then disappear with the realization of the highest.

We must not be thinking of food all the twenty-four hours of the day. The only thing needful is perpetual vigilance, which will help us to find out very soon when we eat for self-indulgence, and when in order only to sustain the body. This being discovered, we must resolutely set our faces against mere indulgence. A common kitchen where this principle is observed is very helpful as it relieves us from the necessity of thinking out the menu for each day, and provides us with acceptable food of which we may take only a limited quantity with a contented and thankful mind. The authorities of a common kitchen lighten our burden and serve as watch-dogs of our observance. They will not pamper us, they will cook only such food as helps us to keep the body a fit instrument for service. In an ideal state, the sun should be our only cook. But I know that we are far, far away from that happy state.

Non-Stealing

We now come to the observance of Non-stealing. Like the last two, this is also implicit in truth. Love maybe deduced from truth, or may be paired with truth. Truth and love are one and the same thing. I am partial to truth however. In the final analysis there can only be a single reality. The highest truth stands by itself. Truth is the end, love a means thereto. We know what is love or non-violence, although we find it difficult to follow the law of love. But as for truth we know only a fraction of it. Perfect knowledge of truth is difficult of attainment for man even like the perfect practice of non-violence.

It is impossible that a person should steal, and simultaneously claim to know truth or cherish love. Yet every one of us is consciously or unconsciously more or less guilty of theft. We may steal not only what belongs to others, but also what belongs to ourselves, as is done, for instance, by a father who eats something secretly, keeping his children in the dark about it. The ashram kitchen stores are our common property, but one who secretly removes a single crystal of sugar from it stamps himself a thief. It is theft to take anything belonging to another without his permission, even if it be with his knowledge. It is equally theft to take something in the belief that it is nobody's property. Things found on the roadside belong to the ruler or the local authority. Anything found near the ashram must be handed over to the secretary, who in his turn will pass it on to the police if it is not ashram property.

Thus far it is pretty smooth sailing. But the observance of non-stealing goes very much farther. It is theft to take something from another even with his permission if we have no real need of it. We should not receive any single thing that we do not need. Theft of this description generally has food for its object. It is theft for me to take any fruit that I do not need, or to take it in a larger quantity than is necessary. We are not always aware of our real needs, and most of us improperly multiply our wants, and thus unconsciously make thieves of ourselves. If we devote some thought to the subject, we shall find that we can get rid of quite a number of our wants. One who follows the observance of non-stealing will bring about a progressive reduction of his own wants. Much of the distressing poverty in this world has arisen out of breaches of the principle of non-stealing.

Theft, thus far considered, may be termed external or physical theft. There is besides another kind of theft subtler and far more degrading to the human spirit. It is theft mentally to desire acquisition of anything belonging to others, or to cast a greedy eye on it. One who takes no food, physically speaking, is generally said to be fasting, but he is guilty of theft, as well as a breach of his fast, if he gives himself up to a mental contemplation of pleasure when he sees others taking their meals. He is similarly guilty if, during his fast, he is continually planning the varied menu he will have after breaking the fast.

One who observes the principle of non-stealing will refuse to bother himself about things to be acquired in the future. This evil anxiety for the future will be found at the root of many a theft. Today we only desire possession of a thing; tomorrow we shall begin to adopt measures, straight if possible, crooked when thought necessary, to acquire its possession.

Ideas may be stolen no less than material things. One who egotistically claims to have originated some good idea, which, really speaking, did not originate with him, is guilty of a theft of ideas. Many learned men have committed such theft in the course of world history, and plagiarism is by no means uncommon even today. Supposing, for instance, that I see a new type of spinning wheel in Andhra and manufacture a similar wheel in the ashram, passing it off as my own invention. I practice untruth, and am clearly guilty of stealing another's invention.

One who takes up the observance of non-stealing has therefore to be humble, vigilant and in habits simple.

Non-Possession

Non-possession is allied to non-stealing. A thing not originally stolen must nevertheless be classified as stolen property, if we possess it without needing it. Possession implies provision for the future. A seeker after truth, a follower of the law of love, cannot hold anything against tomorrow. God never stores for the morrow; he never creates more than what is strictly needed for the moment. If therefore we repose faith in his providence, we should rest assured that he will give us every day our daily bread, meaning everything that we require. Saints and devotees who have lived in such faith have always derived a justification for it from their experience.

Our ignorance or negligence of the divine law, which gives to man from day to day his daily bread and no more, has given rise to inequalities with all the miseries attendant upon them. The rich have a superfluous store of things which they do not need, and which are therefore neglected and wasted, while millions are starved to death for want of sustenance. If each retained possession only of what he needed, no one would be in want, and all would live in contentment. As it is, the rich are discontented no less than the poor. The poor man would fain become a millionaire, and the millionaire a multimillionaire. The rich should take the initiative in dispossession with a view to a universal diffusion of the spirit of contentment. If only they keep their own property within moderate limits, the starving will be easily fed, and will learn the lesson of contentment along with the rich.

Perfect fulfillment of the ideal of non-possession requires that man should, like the birds, have no roof over his head, no clothing, and no stock of food for the morrow. He will indeed need his daily bread, but it will be God's business, and not his, to provide it. Only the fewest possible, if any at all, can reach this ideal. We ordinary seekers may not be repelled by the seeming impossibility. But we must keep the ideal constantly in view, and in the light thereof, critically examine our possessions and try to reduce them. Civilization, in the real sense of the term, consists not in the multiplication, but in the deliberate and voluntary reduction of wants. This alone promotes real happiness and contentment, and increases the capacity for service. Judging by this criterion, we find that in the ashram we possess many things, the necessity for which cannot be proved, and we thus tempt our neighbors to thieve.

From the standpoint of pure truth, the body too is a possession. It has been truly said that desire for enjoyment creates bodies for the soul. When this desire vanishes, there remains no further need for the body, and man is free from the vicious cycle of births and deaths. The soul is omnipresent; why should she care to be confined within the cagelike body, or do evil and even kill for the sake of that cage? We thus arrive at the ideal of total renunciation, and learn to use the body for the purposes of service so long as it exists, so much so that service, and not bread, becomes with us the stuff of life. We eat and drink, sleep and wake, for service alone. Such an attitude of mind brings us real happiness, and the beatific vision in the fullness of time. Let us all examine ourselves from this standpoint.

We should remember, that non-possession is a principle applicable to thoughts, as well as to things. A man who fills his brain with useless knowledge violates that inestimable principle. Thoughts which turn us away from God, or do not turn us towards Him, constitute impediments in our way. In this connection we may consider the definition of knowledge contained in the thirteenth chapter of the *Gita*. We are there told that humility, *amanitvam*, etc. constitute knowledge, and all the rest is ignorance. If this is true—and there is no doubt that it is true—much that we hug today as knowledge is ignorance pure and simple, and therefore only does us harm, instead of conferring any benefit. It makes the mind wander, and even reduces it to a vacuity, and discontent flourishes in endless ramifications of evil.

Needless to say, this is not a plea for inertia. Every moment of our life should be filled with mental or physical activity, but that activity should be *sattvika*, tending to truth. One who has consecrated his life to service cannot be idle for a single moment. But we have to learn to distinguish between good activity and evil activity. This discernment goes naturally with a single-minded devotion to service.

Fearlessness

Every reader of the *Gita* knows that fearlessness heads the list of the divine attributes enumerated in the sixteenth chapter. Whether this is merely due to the exigencies of meter, or whether the pride of place has been deliberately yielded to fearlessness, is more than I can say. In my opinion, however, fearlessness richly deserves the first rank assigned to it. For, it is indispensable for the growth of the other noble qualities. How can one seek truth, or cherish love, without fearlessness? As Pritam says, "The path of Hari, the Lord, is the path of the brave, not of cowards." Hari here means truth, and the brave are those armed with fearlessness, not with the sword, the rifle and the like. These are taken up only by those who are possessed by fear.

Fearlessness connotes freedom from all external fear— fear of disease, bodily injury, death, of dispossession, of losing one's nearest and dearest, of losing reputation or giving offense, and so on. One who overcomes the fear of death does not surmount all other fears, as is commonly but erroneously supposed. Some of us do not fear death, but flee from the minor ills of life. Some are ready to die themselves, but cannot bear their loved ones being taken away from them. Some misers will put up with all this, will part even with their lives, but not their property; others will do any number of black deeds in order to uphold their supposed prestige. Some will swerve from the strait and narrow path, which lies clear before them, simply because they are afraid of incurring the world's odium. The seeker after truth must conquer all these fears. He should be ready to sacrifice his all in the quest of truth, even as Harishchandra did. The story of Harishchandra may be only a parable, but every seeker will bear witness to its truth from his personal experience, and therefore that story is as precious as any historical fact.

Perfect fearlessness can be attained only by him who has realized the Supreme, as it implies freedom from delusions. One can always progress towards this goal by determined and constant endeavor, and by cultivating self-confidence.

As I have stated at the very outset, we must give up all

external fears. But the internal foes we must also fear. We are rightly afraid of animal passion, anger, and the like. External fears cease of their own accord, when once we have conquered these traitors within the camp. All such fears revolve round the body as the center, and will therefore disappear as soon as we get rid of attachment for the body. We thus find that all external fear is the baseless fabric of our own vision. Fear has no place in our hearts when we have shaken off attachment for wealth, for family and for the body. "Enjoy the things of the earth by renouncing them," is a noble precept. Wealth, family and body will be there, just the same; we have only to change our attitude towards them. All these are not ours, but God's.

Nothing whatever in this world is ours. Even we ourselves are his. Why then should we entertain any fears? The Upanishad therefore directs us to "give up attachment for things, while we enjoy them." That is to say, we must be interested in them not as proprietors, but only as trustees. He on whose behalf we hold them will give us the strength and the weapons requisite for defending them against all usurpers. When we thus cease to be masters and reduce ourselves to the rank of servants, humbler than the very dust under our feet, all fears will roll away like mists. We shall attain ineffable peace, and see *Satyanarayan*, the God of truth, face to face.

Removal of Untouchability

This, too, is a new observance, like control of the palate, and may even appear a little strange. But it is of vital importance. Untouchability means pollution by the touch of certain persons by reason of their birth in a particular state or family. In the words of Akha, it is an excrescence. In the guise of religion, it is always in the way, and corrupts religion.

None can be born untouchable, as all are sparks of one and the same fire. It is wrong to treat certain human beings as untouchables from birth. It is also wrong to entertain false scruples about touching a dead body, which should be an object of pity and respect. It is only out of considerations of health that we bathe after handling a dead body, or after an application of oil, or a shave. A man who does not bathe in such cases may be looked upon as dirty, but surely not as a sinner. A mother, may be "untouchable" so long as she has not bathed, or washed her hands and feet, after cleaning up her child's mess, but if a child happened to touch her, it would not be polluted by the touch.

But *Bhangis, Dhedhs, Chamars* and the like are contemptuously looked down upon as untouchables from birth. They may bathe for years with any amount of soap, dress well and wear the marks of *Vaishnavas*, read the *Gita* every day and follow a learned profession, and yet they remain untouchables. This is rank irreligion fit only to be destroyed. By treating removal of untouchability as an ashram observance, we assert our belief that untouchability is not only not a part and parcel of Hinduism, but a plague, which it is the bounden duty of every Hindu to combat. Every Hindu, therefore, who considers it a sin, should atone for it by fraternizing with untouchables, associating with them in a spirit of love and service, deeming himself purified by such acts, redressing their grievances, helping them patiently to overcome ignorance and other evils due to the slavery of ages, and inspiring other Hindus to do likewise.

When one visualizes the removal of untouchability from this spiritual standpoint, its material and political results sink into insignificance, and we befriend the so-called untouchables regardless of such results. Seekers after truth will never waste a thought on the material consequences of their quest, which is not a matter of policy with them, but something interwoven with the very texture of their lives.

When we have realized the supreme importance of this observance, we shall discover that the evil it seeks to combat is not restricted in its operation to the suppressed classes. Evil no bigger than a mustard seed in the first instance soon assumes gigantic proportions, and in the long run destroys that upon which it settles. Thus this evil has now assailed all departments of life. We have hardly enough time even to look after ourselves, thanks to the never ending ablutions and exclusive preparation of food necessitated by false notions of untouchability. While pretending to pray to God, we offer worship not to God, but to ourselves.

This observance, therefore, is not fulfilled merely by making friends with "untouchables," but by loving all life as our own selves. Removal of untouchability means love for, and service of, the whole world, and thus merges into ahimsa. Removal of untouchability spells the breaking down of barriers between man and man, and between the various orders of being. We find such barriers erected everywhere in the world, but here we have been mainly concerned with the untouchability which has received religious sanction in India, reducing many human beings to a state bordering on slavery.

Bread Labor

The law that to live man must work first came home to me upon reading Tolstoy's writing on bread labor. But even before that I had begun to pay homage to it after reading Ruskin's

Unto This. Last. The divine law that man must earn his bread by laboring with his own hands was first stressed by a Russian writer named T. M Bondareff. Tolstoy advertised it and gave it wider publicity. In my view, the same principle has been set forth in the third chapter of the *Gita,* where we are told, that he who eats without offering sacrifice eats stolen food. Sacrifice here can only mean bread labor.

Reason too leads us to an identical conclusion. How can a man who does not do body labor have the right to eat? "In the sweat of thy brow shalt thou eat thy bread," says the Bible. A millionaire cannot carry on for long, and will soon get tired of his life, if he rolls in his bed all day long and is even helped to his food. He therefore induces hunger by exercise, and helps himself to the food he eats. If every one, whether rich or poor, has thus to take exercise in some shape or form, why should it not assume the form of productive, i. e. bread labor?

No one asks the cultivator to take breathing exercise or to work his muscles. And more than nine-tenths of humanity lives by tilling the soil. How much happier, healthier and more peaceful would the world become if the remaining tenth followed the example of the overwhelming majority, at least to the extent of laboring enough for their food! And many hardships connected with agriculture would be easily redressed if such people took a hand in it. Again invidious distinctions of rank would be abolished when every one, without exception, acknowledged the obligation of bread labor. It is common to all the *varnas.* There is a world-wide conflict between capital and labor, and the poor envy the rich. If all worked for their bread, distinctions of rank would be obliterated; the rich would still be there, but they would deem themselves only trustees of their property, and would use it mainly in the public interests

Bread labor is a veritable blessing to one who would observe non-violence, worship truth, and make the observance of *brahmacharya* a natural act. This labor can truly be related to agriculture alone. But at present at any rate, everybody is not in a position to take to it. A person can therefore spin or weave, or take up carpentry or smithery, instead of tilling the soil, always regarding agriculture however to be the ideal.

Every one must be his own scavenger. Evacuation is as necessary as eating; and the best thing would be for every one to dispose of his own waste. If this is impossible, each family should see to its own scavenging. I have felt for years that there must be something radically wrong where scavenging has been made the concern of a separate class in society. We have no historical record of the man who first assigned the lowest status to this essential sanitary service. Whoever he was, he by no means did us a good. We should, from our very childhood, have the idea impressed upon our minds that we are all scavengers, and the easiest way of doing so is, for every one who has realized this to commence bread labor as a scavenger. Scavenging, thus intelligently taken up, will help one to a true appreciation of the equality of man.

Tolerance or Equality of Religions

I do not like the word tolerance, but could not think of a better one. Tolerance may imply a gratuitous assumption of the inferiority of other faiths to one's own, whereas ahimsa teaches us to entertain the same respect for the religious faiths of others as we accord to our own, thus admitting the imperfection of the latter.

This admission will be readily made by a seeker of truth,

who follows the law of love. If we had attained the full vision of truth, we would no longer be mere seekers, but would have become one with God, for truth is God. But being only seekers, we prosecute our quest, and are conscious of our imperfection. And if we are imperfect ourselves, religion as conceived by us must also be imperfect. We have not realized religion in its perfection, even as we have not realized God. Religion of our conception, being thus imperfect, is always subject to a process of evolution and re-interpretation. Progress towards truth, towards God, is possible only because of such evolution. And if all faiths outlined by men are imperfect, the question of comparative merit does not arise. All faiths constitute a revelation of truth, but all are imperfect and liable to error. Reverence for other faiths need not blind us to their faults. We must be keenly alive to the defects of our own faith also, yet not leave it on that account, but try to overcome those defects. Looking at all religions with an equal eye, we would not only not hesitate, but would think it our duty, to blend into our faith every acceptable feature of other faiths.

The question then arises, Why should there be so many different faiths? The soul is one, but the bodies which she animates are many. We cannot reduce the number of bodies; yet we recognize the unity of the soul. Even as a tree has a single trunk but many branches and leaves, so is there one true and perfect religion, but it becomes many as it passes through the human medium. The one religion is beyond all speech. Imperfect men put it into such language as they can command, and their words are interpreted by other men equally imperfect. Whose interpretation is to be held to be the right one? Everybody is right from his own standpoint, but it is not impossible that everybody is wrong. Hence the necessity for tolerance, which does not mean indifference towards one's own faith, but a more intelligent and purer love for it. Tolerance gives us spiritual insight, which is as far from fanaticism as the north pole from the south. True knowledge of religion breaks down the barriers between faith and faith. Cultivation of tolerance for other faiths will impart to us a truer understanding of our own.

Tolerance obviously does not disturb the distinction between right and wrong, or good and evil. The reference here throughout is naturally to the principal faiths of the world. They are all based on common fundamentals. They have all produced great saints.

Tolerance or Equality of Religions II

I would linger yet a while on tolerance. My meaning will perhaps become clearer if I describe here some of my experiences. In Phoenix we had our daily prayers in the same way as in Sabarmati, and Mussalmans as well as Christians attended them along with Hindus. The late Sheth Rustomji and his children, too, frequented the prayer meetings. Rustomji Sheth very much liked the Gujarati *bhajan, Mane valun,* "Dear, dear to me is the name of Rama." If my memory serves me right, Maganlal or Kashi was once leading us in singing this hymn, when Rustomji Sheth exclaimed joyously, "Say the name of Hormazd instead of the name of Rama." His suggestion was readily taken up, and after that whenever the Sheth was present, and sometimes even when he was not, we put in the name of Hormazd in place of Rama.

The late Husain, son of Daud Sheth, often stayed at the Phoenix Ashram, and enthusiastically joined our prayers. To the accompaniment of an organ, he used to sing in a very sweet voice the song, *Hai bahare bagh,* "The garden of this world has only a momentary bloom." He taught us all this song, which we also sang at prayers. Its inclusion in our *Bhajanavali is* a tribute to truth-loving Husain's memory. I have never met a young man who practiced truth more devotedly than Husain. Joseph Royeppen often came to Phoenix. He is a Christian and his favorite hymn was *Vaishnava jana,* "He is *a Vaishnava* (servant of the Lord), who succors people in distress." He loved music and once sang this hymn, saying "Christian" in place of *"Vaishnava."* The others accepted his reading with alacrity, and I observed that this filled Joseph's heart with joy.

When I was turning over the pages of the sacred books of different faiths for my own satisfaction, I became sufficiently familiar for my purpose with Christianity, Islam, Zoroastrianism, Judaism and Hinduism. In reading these texts, I can say that I was equiminded towards all these faiths, although perhaps I was not then conscious of it. Refreshing my memory of those days, I do not find I ever had the slightest desire to criticize any of those religions merely because they were not my own, but read each sacred book in a spirit of reverence, and found the same fundamental morality in each. Some things I did not understand then, and do not understand even now, but experience has taught me that it is a mistake hastily to imagine that anything that we cannot understand is necessarily wrong. Some things which I did not understand at first have since become as clear as daylight. Equimindedness helps us to solve many difficulties, and even when we criticize anything, we express ourselves with a humility and a courtesy which leave no sting behind them.

The acceptance of the doctrine of equality of religions

does not abolish the distinction between religion and irreligion. We do not propose to cultivate toleration for irreligion. That being so, some people might object that there would be no room left for equimindedness if every one took his own decision as to what was religion and what was irreligion. If we follow the law of love, we shall not bear any hatred towards the irreligious brother. On the contrary, we shall love him, and therefore either we shall bring him to see the error of his ways, or he will point out our error, or each will tolerate the other's difference of opinion. If the other party does not observe the law of love, he may be violent to us. If, however, we cherish real love for him, it will overcome his bitterness in the end. All obstacles in our path will vanish if only we observe the golden rule—that we must not be impatient with those whom we may consider to be in error, but must be prepared, if need be, to suffer in our own person.

Humility

Humility cannot be an observance by itself. For it does not lend itself to being deliberately practiced. It is however an indispensable test of ahimsa. In one who has ahimsa in him, it becomes part of his very nature.

A preliminary draft of the rules and regulations of the Satyagraha Ashram was circulated among friends, including the late Sir Gurudas Banerji. He suggested that humility should be accorded a place among the observances. This suggestion could not then be accepted for the reason that I have just mentioned.

But although humility is not one of the observances, it is certainly as essential as, and perhaps even more essential, than any of them. Only it has never come to any one by practice. Truth can be cultivated as well as love. But to cultivate humility is tantamount to cultivating hypocrisy. Humility must not be here confounded with mere manners or etiquette. One man will sometimes prostrate himself before another, although his heart is full of bitterness against him. This is not humility, but cunning. A man may repeat Ramanama, or tell his beads all day long, and move in society like a sage; but if he is selfish at heart, he is not meek but only hypocritical.

A humble person is not himself conscious of his humility. Truth and the like perhaps admit of measurement, but not humility. Inborn humility can never remain hidden, and yet the possessor is unaware of its existence. The story of Vasishtha and Vishvamitra furnishes a very good case in point. Humility should make the possessor realize that he is as nothing. Directly we imagine ourselves to be something, there is egotism. If a man who keeps observances is proud of keeping them, they will lose much, if not all of their value. And a man who is proud of his virtue often becomes a curse to society. Society will not appreciate it, and he himself will fail to reap any benefit from it.

Only a little thought will suffice to convince us that all creatures are nothing more than a mere atom in this universe. Our existence as embodied beings is purely momentary; what are a hundred years in eternity! But if we shatter the chains of egotism and melt into the ocean of humanity, we share its dignity. To feel that we are something is to set up a barrier between God and ourselves; to cease feeling that we are something is to become one with God. A drop in the ocean partakes of the greatness of its parent, although it is unconscious of it. But it is dried up as soon as it enters upon an existence independent of the ocean. We do not exaggerate when we say that life on earth is a mere bubble.

A life of service must be one of humility. He who would sacrifice his life for others has hardly time to reserve for himself a place in the sun. Inertia must not be mistaken for humility, as it has been in Hinduism. True humility means most strenuous and constant endeavor entirely directed towards the service of humanity. God is continuously in action without resting for a single moment. If we would serve him or become one with him, our activity must be as unwearied as his. There may be momentary rest in store for the drop which is separated from the ocean, but not for the drop in the ocean, which knows no rest. The same is the case with ourselves. As soon as we become one with the ocean in the shape of God, there is no more rest for us, nor indeed do we need rest any longer. Our very sleep is action. For we sleep with the thought of God in our hearts. This restlessness constitutes true rest.

This never-ceasing agitation holds the key to peace ineffable. This supreme state of total surrender is difficult to describe but not beyond the bounds of human experience. It has been attained by many dedicated souls and may be attained by ourselves as well. This is the goal which we of the Satyagraha Ashram set before ourselves; all our observances and activities are calculated to assist us in reaching it. We shall reach it some day all unawares if we have the truth in us.

The Importance of Vows

In this series I have dealt cursorily with the importance of vows, but it is perhaps necessary to consider at some length their bearing on a godly life. There is a powerful school of thinkers, who concede the propriety of observing certain rules, but do not acknowledge the necessity of vows. They go even so far as to suggest that vows are a sign of weakness, and may even be harmful. Again they argue, that if a rule is subsequently discovered to be inconvenient or sinful, to adhere to it after such discovery would be positively wrong. They say it is a good thing to abstain from liquor, but what harm is there in taking it occasionally, say on medical grounds? A pledge of total abstinence, would be a needless handicap; and as with liquor, so with other things.

A vow means unflinching determination, and helps us against temptations. Determination is worth nothing if it bends before discomfort. The universal experience of humanity supports the view that progress is impossible without inflexible determination. There cannot be a vow to commit a sin; in the case of a vow first thought to be meritorious but later found to be sinful, there arises a clear necessity to give it up. But no one takes, or ought to take, vows about dubious matters. Vows can be taken only on points of universally recognized principles. The possibility of sin in such a case is more or less imaginary.

A devotee of truth cannot stop to consider if some one will not be injured by his telling the truth, for he believes that truth can never do harm. So also about total abstinence. The abstainer will either make an exception as regards medicine, or will be prepared to risk his life in fulfillment of his full vow. What does it matter if we happen to lose our lives through a pledge of total abstinence? There can be no guarantee that our lives will be prolonged by liquor, and even if life is thus prolonged for a moment, it may be ended the very next through some other agency. On the other hand, the example of a man who gives up his life rather than his pledge is likely to wean drunkards from liquor, and thus become a great power for good in the world. Only they can hope some time to see God who have nobly determined to bear witness to the faith that is in them, even at the cost of life itself.

Taking vows is not a sign of weakness, but of strength. To do at any cost something that one ought to do constitutes a vow. It becomes a bulwark of strength. A man who says that he will do something "as far as possible" betrays either his pride or his weakness. I have noticed in my own case, as well as in the case of others, that the limitation "as far as possible" provides a fatal loophole. To do something as far as possible is to succumb to the very first temptation. There is no sense in saying that we will observe truth as far as possible. Even as no businessman will look at a note in which a man promises to pay a certain amount on a certain date "as far as possible," so will God refuse to accept a promissory note drawn by a man who will observe truth as far as possible.

God is the very image of the vow. God would cease to be God if he swerved from his own laws even by a hair's breadth. The sun is a great keeper of observances; hence the possibility of measuring time and publishing almanacs. All business depends upon men fulfilling their promises. Are such promises less necessary in character building or self-realization? We should therefore never doubt the necessity of vows for the purpose of self-purification and self-realization.

Yajna or Sacrifice

Yajna means an act directed to the welfare of others, done without desiring any return for it, whether of a temporal or spiritual nature. "Act" here must be taken in its widest sense, and includes thought and word as well as deed. "Others" embraces not only humanity, but all life. Therefore, and also from the standpoint of ahimsa, it is not a yajna to sacrifice lower animals even with a view to the service of humanity. It does not matter that animal sacrifice is alleged to find a place in the Vedas. It is enough for us that such sacrifice cannot stand the fundamental tests of truth and non-violence. I readily admit my incompetence in Vedic scholarship. But the incompetence so far as this subject is concerned does not worry me, because even if the practice of animal sacrifice be proved to have been a feature of Vedic society, it can form no precedent for a votary of ahimsa.

Again a primary sacrifice must be an act which conduces the most to the welfare of the greatest number in the widest area, and which can be performed by the largest number of men and women with the least trouble. It will not therefore, be a yajna much less a mahayajna, to wish or to do ill to any one else, even in order to serve a so-called higher interest. And the *Gita* teaches, and experience testifies, that all action that cannot come under the category of yajna promotes bondage.

The world cannot subsist for a single moment without yajna in this sense, and therefore the *Gita*, after having dealt with true wisdom in the second chapter, takes up in the third the means of attaining it, and declares in so many words that yajna came with the creation itself. This body therefore has been given us only in order that we may serve all creation with it. And therefore, says the *Gita*, he who eats without offering yajna eats stolen food. Every single act of one who would lead a life of purity should be in the nature of yajna. Yajna having come to us with our birth, we are debtors all our lives, and thus for ever bound to serve the universe. And even as a bondslave receives food, clothing and so on from the master whom he serves, so should we gratefully accept such gifts as may be assigned to us by the lord of the universe.

What we receive must be called a gift; for as debtors we are entitled to no consideration for the discharge of our obligations. Therefore we may not blame the master if we fail to get it. Our body is his to be cherished or cast away according to his will. This is not a matter for complaint or even pity; on the contrary, it is a natural and even a pleasant and desirable state, if only we realize our proper place in God's scheme. We do indeed need strong faith if we would experience this supreme bliss. "Do not worry in the least about yourself, leave all worry to God." This appears to be the commandment in all religions.

This need not frighten any one. He who devotes himself to service with a clear conscience will day-by-day grasp the necessity for it in greater measure, and will continually grow richer in faith. The path of service can hardly be trodden by one who is not prepared to renounce self-interest and to recognize the conditions of his birth. Consciously or unconsciously every one of us does render some service or other. If we cultivate the habit of doing this service deliberately, our desire for service will steadily grow stronger, and will make not only for our own happiness, but that of the world at large.

More About Yajna

I wrote about *yajna* last week, but feel like writing more about it. It will perhaps be worth while further to consider a principle which has been created along with mankind. Yajna is duty to be performed, or service to be rendered, all the twenty-four hours of the day. To serve without desire is to favor not others, but ourselves, even as in discharging a debt we serve only ourselves, lighten our burden and fulfill our duty. Again not only the good, but all of us are bound to place our resources at the disposal of humanity. And if such is the law, as evidently it is, indulgence ceases to hold a place in life and gives way to renunciation. The duty of renunciation differentiates mankind from the beast.

Some object that life thus understood becomes dull and devoid of art, and leaves no room for the householder. But renunciation here does not mean abandoning the world and retiring into the forest. The spirit of renunciation should rule all the activities of life. A householder does not cease to be one if he regards life as a duty rather than is an indulgence. A merchant who operates in the sacrificial spirit will have [tens of thousands] passing through his bands, but he will, if he follows the law, use his abilities for service. He will therefore not cheat or speculate, will lead a simple life, will not injure a living soul and will lose millions rather than harm anybody.

Let no one run away with the idea that this type of merchant exists only in my imagination. Fortunately for the world, it does exist in the West as well as in the East. It is true, such merchants may be counted on one's fingers' ends, but the type ceases to be imaginary as soon as even one living specimen can be found to answer to it. All of us know of a philanthropic tailor in Wadhwan. I know of one such barber. Every one of us knows such a weaver. And if we go deeply into the matter, we shall come across men in every walk of life who lead dedicated lives. No doubt these sacrificers obtain their livelihood by their work. But livelihood is not their objective, but only a by-product of their vocation. Motilal was a tailor at first and continued as tailor afterwards. But his spirit was changed and his work was transmuted into worship. He began to think about the welfare of others, and his life became artistic in the real sense of the term.

A life of sacrifice is the pinnacle of art, and is full of true joy. Yajna is not yajna if one feels it to be burdensome or annoying. Self-indulgence leads to destruction, and renunciation to immortality. Joy has no independent existence. It depends upon our attitude to life. One man will enjoy theatrical scenery, another the ever new scenes which unfold themselves in the sky. Joy, therefore, is a matter of individual and national education. We shall delight in things which we have been taught to delight in as children. And illustrations can be easily cited of different national tastes.

Again, many sacrificers imagine that they are free to receive from the people everything they need, and many things they do not need, because they are rendering disinterested service. Directly this idea sways a man, he ceases to be a servant and becomes a tyrant over the people.

One who would serve will not waste a thought upon his own comforts, which he leaves to be attended to, or neglected by, his master on high. He will not therefore encumber himself with everything that comes his way; he will take only what he strictly needs and leave the rest. He will be calm, free from anger and unruffled in mind even if he finds himself inconvenienced. His service, like virtue, is its own reward, and he will rest content with it.

Again one dare not be negligent in service, or be behindhand with it. He who thinks that he must be diligent only in his personal business, and unpaid public business may be done in any way and at any time he chooses, has still to learn the very rudiments of the science of sacrifice. Voluntary service of others demands the best of which one is capable, and must take precedence over service of self. In fact, the pure devotee consecrates himself to the service of humanity without any reservation whatever.

Swadeshi

Note: This essay on swadeshi was not written in Yeravda Central Prison in 1930, but outside, after Gandhiji's release in 1931. He did not write it in jail, as he felt he would perhaps be unable to do justice to the subject without encroaching upon the forbidden field of politics. The translation was done by Shri Pyarelal.

Swadeshi is the law of laws enjoined by the present age. Spiritual laws, like nature's laws, need no enacting; they are self-acting. But through ignorance or other causes man often neglects or disobeys them. It is then that vows are needed to steady his course. A man who is by temperament a vegetarian needs no vow to strengthen his vegetarianism. For the sight of animal food, instead of tempting him, would only excite his disgust. The law of swadeshi is ingrained in the basic nature of man, but it has today sunk into oblivion. Hence the necessity for the vow of swadeshi.

In its ultimate and spiritual sense, swadeshi stands for the final emancipation of the soul from her earthly bondage. For this earthly tabernacle is not her natural or permanent abode; it is a hindrance in her onward journey; it stands in the way of her realizing her oneness with all life. A votary of swadeshi, therefore, in his striving to identify himself with the entire creation, seeks to be emancipated from the bondage of the physical body.

If this interpretation of swadeshi be correct, then it follows, that its votary will, as a first duty, dedicate himself to the service of his immediate neighbors, This involves exclusion or even sacrifice of the interests of the rest, but the exclusion or the sacrifice would be only in appearance. Pure service of our neighbors can never, from its very nature, result in disservice to those who are far away, but rather the contrary. "As with the individual, so with the universe" is an unfailing principle, which we would do well to lay to heart. On the other hand, a man who allows himself to be lured by "the distant scene," and runs to the ends of the earth for service, is not only foiled in his ambition, but also falls in his duty towards his neighbors.

Take a concrete instance. In the particular place where I live, I have certain persons as my neighbors, some relations and dependents. Naturally, they all feel, as they have a right to, that they have a claim on me, and look to me for help and support. Suppose now I leave them all at once, and set out to serve people in a distant place. My decision would throw my little world of neighbors and dependents out of gear, while my gratuitous knight-errantry would, more likely than not, disturb the atmosphere in the new place. Thus a culpable neglect of my immediate neighbors, and an unintended disservice to the people whom I wish to serve, would be the first fruits of my violation of the principles of swadeshi.

It is not difficult to multiply such instances. That is why the Gita says, "It is best to die performing one's own duty or *svadharma; paradharma* or another's duty is fraught with danger." Interpreted in terms of one's physical environment, this gives

155

us the law of swadeshi. What the *Gita* says with regard to *svadharma* equally applies to swadeshi, for swadeshi is *svadharma* applied to one's immediate environment.

It is only when the doctrine of swadeshi is wrongly understood that mischief results. For instance, it would be a travesty of the doctrine of swadeshi, if, to coddle my family, I set about grabbing money by all means fair or foul. The law of swadeshi requires no more of me than to discharge my legitimate obligations towards my family by just means, and the attempt to do so will reveal to me the universal code of conduct. The practice of swadeshi can never do harm to any one, and if it does, it is not *svadharma* but egotism that moves me.

There may arise occasions, when a votary of swadeshi may be called upon to sacrifice his family at the altar of universal service. Such an act of willing immolation will then constitute the highest service rendered to the family. "Whosoever saveth his life shall lose it, and whosoever loseth his life for the Lord's sake shall find it" holds good for the family group no less than for the individual. Take another instance. Supposing there is an outbreak of plague in my village, and in trying to serve the victims of the epidemic, I, my wife and children, and all the rest of my family are wiped out of existence; then in inducing those dearest and nearest to join me, I will not have acted as the destroyer of my family, but on the contrary as its truest friend. In swadeshi there is no room for selfishness; or if there is selfishness in it, it is of the highest type, which is not different from the highest altruism. Swadeshi in its purest form is the acme of universal service.

It was by following this line of argument, that I hit upon khadi as the necessary and the most important corollary of the principle of swadeshi in its application to society. "What is the kind of service," I asked myself, "that the teeming millions of India most need at the present time, that can be easily understood and appreciated by all, that is easy to perform, and will, at the same time, enable the [tens of thousands] of our semi-starved countrymen to live?" And the reply came, that it is the universalizing of khadi, or the spinning-wheel alone, that can fulfill these conditions.

Let no one suppose, that the practice of swadeshi through khadi would harm the foreign or Indian mill owners. A thief who is weaned from his vice, or is made to return the property that he has stolen, is not harmed thereby. On the contrary, he is the gainer, consciously in the one case, unconsciously in the other. Similarly, if all the opium addicts or drunkards in the world were to shake themselves free from their vice, the canteen keepers or the opium vendors, who would be-deprived of their custom could not be said to be losers. They would be the gainers in the truest sense of the word. The elimination of the wages of sin is never a loss either to the individual concerned or to society; it is pure gain.

It is the greatest delusion to suppose that the duty of swadeshi begins and ends with merely spinning some yarn anyhow and wearing khadi made from it. Khadi is the first indispensable step towards the discharge of swadeshi *dharma* to society. But one often meets men who wear khadi, while in all other things they indulge their taste for foreign manufactures. Such men cannot be said to be practicing swadeshi. They are simply following the fashion. A votary of swadeshi will carefully study his environment, and try to help his neighbors wherever possible, by giving preference to local manufactures, even if they are of an inferior grade or dearer in price than things manufactured elsewhere. He will try to remedy their defects, but will not because of their defects give them up in favor of foreign manufactures.

But even swadeshi, like any other good thing, can be ridden to death if it is made a fetish. That is a danger which must be guarded against. To reject foreign manufactures merely because they are foreign, and to go on wasting national time and money in the promotion in one's country of manufactures for which it is not suited would be criminal folly, and a negation of the swadeshi spirit. A true votary of swadeshi will never harbor ill-will towards the foreigner; he will not be actuated by antagonism towards anybody on earth. Swadeshism is not a cult of hatred. It is a doctrine of selfless service, that has its roots in the purest ahimsa, i. e. Love.

Contributors

M. K. GANDHI is regarded by many as a Hindu saint and the father of Indian independence. Born at Porbandar on October 2, 1869, he left India as a young man to study law in London. His legal career took him to South Africa in 1893, where he first became involved in political struggles, working to secure rights for Indian expatriates. He remained in South Africa for more than two decades, and it was during these years that his remarkable form of political reform through non-violence, which he called Satyagraha, was born.

Upon his return to India, Gandhi assumed a leadership role in the fight for Indian independence from Great Britain. He also worked tirelessly for religious toleration in India, which was divided by Hindu-Moslem antagonism, and for the destruction of the caste system, which codified class conflicts in ancient religious terms. Gandhi's role emerged not only as that of a political revolutionary, but also as a religious leader. As he insisted, he was a man of God first.

Indian independence from Britain was finally achieved on August 15, 1947. Five months later, on January 25, 1948, Gandhi was assassinated by a conservative Hindu.

MICHAEL N. NAGLER is Professor Emeritus of Classics and Comparative Literature at the University of California, Berkeley. He is the founder of the University's Peace and Conflict Studies Program, and currently teaches courses in nonviolence and meditation. Dr. Nagler is the author of

America Without Violence, and, with Eknath Easwaran, an English edition of *The Upanishads*, as well as numerous articles on classics, myth, peace and mysticism.

ARUN GANDHI is the fifth grandson of Mahatma Gandhi. Raised in South Africa at the Phoenix Ashram, a religious community established by his grandfather in 1904, he moved to India as a teenager in 1945, and lived with the Mahatma during the last years of his life. Dr. Gandhi is a former journalist, and with his wife, Sunanda, started India's Center for Social Unity, an organization dedicated to alleviating poverty and caste discrimination. The author of eight books, Dr. Gandhi has been a resident of the United States since 1987. He and his wife are founders of the M. K. Gandhi Institute for Nonviolence at Christian Brothers University in Memphis, Tennessee.